Having Guests Means Never Seeing the View

Throughout Life
Always Enjoy the
View!
Gayle Haumelin

Having Guests Means Never Seeing the View

Gayle Harmelin

Merryhill Press
Great Barrington, Massachusetts • Boca Raton, Florida

This book is a creative memoir.
The people, incidents, and dialogue herein are drawn from an amalgam of events in which the characters and time frames have enjoyed a liberal interpretation.

HAVING GUESTS MEAN NEVER SEEING THE VIEW

Printed in the United States of America
First Printing

Library of Congress Cataloging-in-Publication Data

Harmelin, Gayle
Having guests means never seeing the view / Gayle Harmelin
Library of Congress Control Number: 2007909447

ISBN 13: 978-0-615-17829-5

Dedicated to Joel, who has been listening to me read and reread versions of this book for what seems like a thousand years.

With many thanks to first readers Gloria Hirsch, Carole Beris, Sandy Kanin, Myrna Lippman, and Jeannie McCallister, who read and critiqued this book with honesty and intelligence.

A very special thank you to Jane Bernstein, my editor and now a dear friend. With each gentle push from her, I was able to realize in print the book that was in my head.

Introduction

Fifteen years ago, shortly after my fiftieth birthday – when I couldn't tell if my future was before me or behind me – I knew it was time for a change. That change took the form of a rented house in the Berkshires. Six years later, my husband Joel and I traded in the rental for home ownership. Our new residence had a spectacular mountain view. A landscape of dense evergreens rose up Monument Mountain, layer upon layer of trees completely bridging the space between earth and sky. But it wasn't too long after guests started to arrive that I realized weekends had become "viewless" days for Joel and me. Weekend after weekend we spent looking at walls and windows as our guests enjoyed the scenery around them. It was with a chuckle that I sat down late one Sunday night and wrote my first story about what it was like to have company – "Having Guests Means Never Seeing the View." I hadn't kept a diary since I was a teenaged girl long ago, though I had never stopped writing – whether it was a story about one of my children, a comical tale about a vacation gone awry, or a couple of thousand recommendations for my high school students applying to college. Writing, for me, has been a cathartic way to be expressive for personal and practical reasons. Our Berkshire life rekindled my desire to start writing a diary. The entries started out as humorous vignettes about the difficulties and delights of having guests. As time went by, the stories became more intense and the reflections of a life, my life, came to occupy the pages of this journal.

My childhood diary was written as the mood dictated. My entries then, and now in the journal you are about to read, are sporadic – sometimes chronicling life weekly, sometimes only monthly, sometimes with gaps of months or even a year or two. The entries reflect true experiences, though I've taken liberties with the time frame in which some of these events took place. Fictitious names replaced real ones where it seemed that some delicacy was required. For these reasons, I would call this diary a creative memoir.

The Appendix is a compendium of all the places of interest in the book. If you go to Berkshire County, and you should, these pages will help you plan your time. You too may get caught by the magic of the Berkshire Hills. Enjoy the journey with me.

Gayle Harmelin
April 2008

Foreword

July 20, 1997

I had been eagerly awaiting the arrival of our first weekend guests. Thoughts of warm welcomes and gracious friends sharing good times, food, and laughter danced in my head like the sugar plum fairies of the Nutcracker Suite. I'm finding, however, that the reality of my role as hostess is a bit more "march" than "ballet." As the weeks roll on, a certain pattern is slowing emerging. Preparation for the next set of guests becomes my weekly occupation, requiring planning comparable to that of a White House state dinner for a visiting dignitary.

Stocking the house with favorite munchies, hmmm, let's see: The Wolffs love their pate. Fred Morton really enjoys blue cheese. I'd better stock up on plenty of Diet Coke for Don Altman. Myra loves her bread and only drinks her vodka with orange slices, while her husband Alan likes his vodka any way you serve it as long as it is Stoli. Then there is the low-fat crowd; better buy salsa and fat-free chips, fat-free cookies, fat-free mayonnaise, Egg Beaters, low-fat margarine, and make-believe cheese – all, I find out later, to be thrown out because they are now on the Atkins diet.

Should I buy Ben & Jerry's Cherry Garcia, Joel's favorite? But don't I remember from last year that the Schactels really loved vanilla from Berkshire Ice Cream? The arrival of more friends stretches my ability to remember if the preferences are for pecan praline swirl – or perhaps mocha nut chocolate? Can't quite recall. OK, buy it all. Buying and shopping. Shopping and buying. Each week a different set of guests with different needs and tastes.

Is the house in order? Better check to see if there is plenty of soap and bathroom tissue. And yes, bottles of spring water and fresh flowers in each guest room.

The Alders and the Millers were supposed to arrive at noon yesterday. Lunch was ready and the farm table on the porch was set. It was a clear summer day. The view of the mountains from our porch was achingly beautiful – that noonday sun, just at its peak, turning the tree tops a golden yellow. That same fiery sun setting off what I call a Provence-blue sky, more like lavender than cornflowers.

12:30. I was so glad they were a bit late. I really needed an extra few minutes, and Joel walked in from the golf course later than expected.

1:00. I began to wonder if my guests had gotten lost. Sometimes my directions get a little confusing. A few weeks ago, I told the Wilsons to head north on Route 23 when it is actually east. For some reason, I always think that if a road goes uphill it must be heading north. Well, I sure found out that wasn't true after the Wilsons told me they ended up in Hudson, New York, before turning around and heading east.

1:30. Given that this is the era of cell phones, I was surprised our expected guests hadn't even called. "Just relax and enjoy the quiet," I told myself, trying to quell the irritation creeping up on me.

Finally, the sound of a car in the driveway announced that our guests had arrived. I greeted them with outstretched arms and a big smile. "I hope I didn't give you the wrong directions," I purred while looking at the clock, which now read 1:40. "Oh no, your directions were perfect. We just got a late start this morning. I guess we really have our vacation mentality in place." I can't say I was really satisfied with that answer, but it would be a long weekend if I didn't just let it go. Which I did.

And as we sat down for lunch, it was apparent that our guests were captivated by the distant views of lush green mountain ranges and deep blue skies, interrupted with only the softest mounds of white clouds drifting peacefully by. I, on the other hand, sat facing the gray clapboard of our house. Aware of their contentment, I was suddenly aware of something else – that having guests means never seeing the view.

The weekend is over, and by 6:00 this evening they had all left. Even Joel returned to New Jersey until Thursday. Most of my friends love that moment when the house is all theirs, the quiet that follows the tumult. I find that watching everyone depart gives me a lonely pit in my stomach. I walked around the house discarding half-dead flowers and empty soda cans. Around 7:30, after eating some leftover chicken, I went onto the porch and even the sun was bidding me goodbye as it slowly dimmed behind the mountains. That familiar aching nostalgia was with me again, pushing me into memories. How did we get to this spot in our lives? What confluence of events finds me here?

I went down to the storage area checking unopened boxes to find my diaries. So many things I cherish seem to get lost as we clean this closet or that basement. Poems the kids wrote, really special poems that I will never see again for the act of some careless discarding of a pile that seemed unimportant at the time. I was ready to give up when I came across a large box filled with old papers and checkbooks. I dug underneath and there they were – diaries from junior high school and high school. Old yearbooks and autograph books. On the very bottom of the pile was the most recent of my diaries, the one I had begun not long ago, the year I turned fifty. A year of life-altering events.

By then the sky was dark, aglow with the stars that seem to blanket the heavens here in the country as in no other place. Diary in hand, I returned to the porch, turned on the light, and began to read.

Part One

August 24, 1990

Mother, who hides her age better than the Pentagon hides its nuclear secrets, keeps telling me not to mention my age. "After all, your age tells a lot about my age," she said last week, "so do me a favor and don't tell." No matter how Mom feels, I cannot deny the obvious. I am turning fifty. I can't believe it – fifty. I thought there was only one dirty F-word. Now there are two. Yes, fifty is my new F-word, and it's talking to me loud and clear. "You ain't no kid no more," it's saying, and while the educator in me wants to correct it to "You are not a child anymore," I know that the truth is raw and "You ain't no kid" says it like it is. My startling age has caused me to be reflective, on the past year especially. I became a grandmother in May. For nine months I watched my daughter enlarge with this wonderful being inside her, and on May 3rd Nancy gave birth to my first grandchild, Danielle Elizabeth. I told Mother that it was awfully hard for me to hide my age or hers when my grown daughter now had a daughter of her own. "And Mom," I said, "that makes you a great-grandmother. How are you going to explain that to your friends?!"

Later we stood in front of the nursery, eyes pressed to the glass, trying to get some sense of the small, beautiful, red-faced child in the plastic crib. All of us, daughter, son-in-law, his parents, my parents, and Joel and me, unable to move from the glass separating us from our newest precious loved one.

A first grandchild. Someone who will have a name for me like nothing I have ever been called before. Grandma. I am the first of my friends to be a grandmother. I am filled with both awe and joy at this miracle which has entered our lives. Her name is a remembrance of two wonderful women, grandmothers in their own time. Danielle Elizabeth is named for my son-in-law's paternal grandmother and for my paternal grandmother, who was an inspiration in my own life.

When I was six years old, Daddy and I stayed with his parents while my newly born sister and my mother stayed with her family. It was an arrangement made necessary in 1945 by the end of the war and a housing shortage. We lived this way for six months until my parents were able to secure a small one-bedroom apartment in Orange, New Jersey.

Those six months in my grandma's house were golden. The house, on Meeker Avenue in Newark, was grand by many standards and absolutely palatial to my young eyes, as we had lived in a two-room, third-floor walk-up prior to this temporary move to my grandparents'.

Their house had three floors and fourteen rooms. The rooms were spacious and furnished for comfort. Behind the living room was a small parlor with family pictures covering all four walls. I stared for many hours at the pictures of younger looking aunts and uncles, as well as relatives I didn't know very well or had never met. Pictures of my mother – considered a great beauty with her dark hair, wide set eyes, and a perfect nose – and of my handsome, athletic father totally captivated my attention. I don't know what ever happened to all the pictures on that wall. All I know is that for me, they have passed into history never to be seen again.

We were not alone in needing living quarters. Joining us in that big house were my aunt and her husband, just home from the war, their son Robert, and my father's youngest brother, as well as both of my grandparents. Dad and I had a room on the second floor, next to Aunt Pearl, Uncle Phil, and my cousin Robert.

Every morning our day started with calisthenics in the front hall. Grandma and Grandpa and Robert and myself, doing knee bends and stretches for about fifteen minutes. I think my grandparents started the fitness craze in that very hall. Every night we went for a long walk to Bergen Street. No matter how cold, this was how the evening ended.

In the mornings, before Dad took me to school, Grandma would make me a milkshake with a raw egg in it. I still gag at the thought, but I know that a lot of love and caring went into this shake. Then she would braid my hair, and off to school I went.

Returning home to Grandma's was always anticipated with delight. She was the best cook and baker ever, and the smell of her cakes and pies coming out of the oven just as I walked in became the scent of all good things to come. Even today as I walk by a bakery and that fresh buttery smell hits my nose, I am transported back to the comfort and safety of Grandma's kitchen – a grand, spanking clean, white-tile affair.

The aromas from Grandma's pots called us to the kitchen table at exactly six o'clock. Grandpa listened to the news as if it were the Ten Commandments coming off Mount Sinai, and no one was allowed to talk while Grandpa was listening. After the news, there was much chatter about the day's events, with grownups talking politics and us kids just listening quietly. After dinner we took our nightly walk, and then bedtime. Sometimes before bed, we would have a most unusual treat. Grandpa would put on the Victrola, which played 78 rpm records. He and Grandma liked to dance, and we would watch them tango around the room, gracefully twirling and dipping to the rhythms of exotic Latin music.

This was life in Grandma's house. Structured but filled with warmth and love. I learned how to live an entire life watching Grandma. To this day, my love of cooking, my love of neatness, my love of nurturing others and making them feel at home in my home are the gifts I received from Grandma during the precious six months Dad and I lived in that house.

I wonder if I can be such an inspiration to Danielle Elizabeth, Grandma's namesake. What a legacy – to have so positive an impact on a younger generation. One day old, and I already loved Danielle as I loved my Grandma. My only question of nature is: Did all if this have to coincide with my first gray hairs? Grandmas and gray hairs seem to be a logical combination. A combination, along with the word fifty, that tells us a new generation is coming into this world.

September 25, 1990

I didn't think this birthday was a big deal. I guess I was wrong, for I find myself consumed with thoughts of time passing at a frightening pace. The future used to be something to aspire to. It was always in front of us. Always beckoning us to accomplish things for some vague and distant time we call the "future." Joel and I worked for the future, he in the stock market and me with varied careers as high school guidance counselor and social worker and then as owner of a gift basket business with our daughter Nancy. We raised our children so that in the future they would be independent adults. We wanted them to be contributors to society, to be kind and caring, to be successful, and to meet a life partner with whom they could then look to their own futures.

Well, guess what, Gayle? For me the future is here. Those of us in my generation have arrived. Essentially, Joel and I have used our opportunities as best we knew how. There were business ventures that failed and business ventures that prospered. We had arguments over golf, money, how to raise our children, and a mass of small things, like me never closing cabinet doors and Joel never giving messages. We negotiated our way through the arguments, managed to have enough money to live comfortably, and now we are proud of all three of our children. As for the other irritations, we are still working on those, but with enough laughter and humor to make the effort worthwhile.

Yes, that F-word is telling me that the future is now. Our fantasies of achieving greatness must be tempered with the knowledge that perhaps we can only achieve modestly. Joel is a talented athlete. He wanted so much to be a great golfer. Not just great at the golf club, but great in state tournaments – and perhaps there has also been the fantasy of national recognition as a touring amateur. He is really, really good, but true greatness has eluded him.

I have yet to figure out my fantasies for greatness. I think I am jealous of Martha Stewart. I love to decorate. I am a fine cook and have always been creative in my home, never needing a decorator to achieve the look that other people seem to admire. If I'm so terrific, how come she is the domestic diva and not I? How come I am not Erma Bombeck? I can be witty about all the mundane oddities that go on in a life on a daily basis. Everybody laughs heartily when I tell a story about the dog eating the four $100 bills I left on the counter for a minute while I had to run to the bathroom. How come I am not Dear Abby? I was a great social worker. I counseled hundreds of parents and kids on the same types of issues she deals with in those columns. These great women have the guts to promote themselves in a big way. Is that what I'm lacking? The guts or confidence to take whatever talents are mine and share them with the world? Maybe the world isn't interested in what I have to offer...

Let's be realistic, Gayle. Now is the time to understand where we are and to appreciate who we are without regrets. After all, even if the future is now, we still have plenty of time to enjoy who we are. We may even surprise ourselves as time moves on. In the spirit of just being ourselves, we may indeed, move from modest achievement to a higher level. The difference is simply to let it happen. Even if this is not the future we once aspired to, it is the present that we must live with. And that's OK with me.

December 12, 1990

At fifty I am ready for some change. I think the impending new year is increasing this urgency. Twenty-five years ago, Joel walked through our front door one warm spring evening and told me he had joined Shackamaxon Country Club. We had two young children then – David was two years old and Nancy, six months old – and we had just moved to a small house in a New Jersey suburb. To say I was dumbfounded by Joel's announcement is a monumental understatement. A country club? What were we doing at a country club at our stage in life? Well, it seemed as if that club was going to be a part of our lives, a part I resisted for a long time. Honestly Gayle, what was so terrible about belonging to a club? It should have been fun. Like Joel said, new people, a new social life, and maybe a chance to play some tennis or golf. I didn't see it that way. What I saw was exactly what happened: Joel playing golf on Saturday and Sunday all spring, summer, and fall. I saw a life at our young age that was contracting instead of expanding.

There were Saturday afternoons when Joel had to throw his hat through the door to see my reaction when he returned home. Eventually, we moved around the corner from the club, a move that probably saved our marriage. The children – three by then with the birth of Mark – and I spent time at the pool with all the other moms and their kids. Joel would come to the pool after golf and play with the kids until dinnertime when all the families would head to the clubhouse for the family barbeque.

Shackamaxon was not your fancy, exclusive country club. Down-to-earth, ordinary people simply enjoyed each other's company. As the kids got older, many of them caddied and made their summer money carrying golf bags. The girls became counselors at the pool's day camp. It turned out to be a wonderful family environment.

The Tepper family was an unexpected benefit. Neal Tepper, the youngest son in this family, was a terrific golfer and would often play with Mark late in the afternoon. Our son was considerably younger than

Neal, but the golf game made the age difference unimportant. Mark liked Neal and thought Neal and his sister Nancy could be a real match. And, as the cliché goes, the rest is history. Without that introduction we would not have our little Danielle. So really good things came out of Joel's poorly received announcement that he had joined a country club.

All of our children are grown, two are married, and the idea of striking out and doing something new appeals to me. Maybe it is a way to feel young again. Getting involved with something new also means staking out a new future, and what is more youthful than reaching for the future as we did when we were kids ourselves? Perhaps a new place. A spot where we might find aspects of ourselves we never knew existed. But where is that place?

We have spent time in the Hamptons. I wonder why that outpost of Eastern Long Island doesn't sink into the ocean. Potato fields that once covered acre upon acre of property have been turned into a sea of dwellings, some boasting 10,000, 15,000, even 20,000 square feet of living space. They are lined up one after the other, competing for the oohs and aahhs of people like us, passersby trying to get more than a tiny glimpse, though their massive chimneys are barely visible behind thirty-foot high hedges. The land may have given up the fields to housing developers, but I've noticed that, subtle as it is, the soil continues to send out the faint odor of potatoes plowed under for the sake of development. I think nature is having a good laugh. I think the Hamptons are not for us.

We have also explored the Jersey Shore. Joel and I have stayed with friends or rented for a summer's week from the coastline of small old towns like Bradley Beach and the more upscale communities of Deal and Long Branch to the more southerly shores of Long Beach Island. Joel is not happy in the sand and often thinks it needs to be surgically removed from his toes and any other part of his anatomy afflicted by the scratchiness of those tiny grains that invariably get imbedded in all sorts of body parts. I know the beach is definitely not going to go over big with Joel.

So looking east isn't going to work and going south isn't ideal. Maybe we should look north to the countryside of western Massachusetts. We have spent wonderful weeks in Lenox, and riding through the Berkshires is an experience different than any of the other places I have thought about. That part of New England has made us feel that we were reliving trips through Ireland and the rural parts of England. Narrow winding roads fronting farms with herds of sheep, cows, and those hairy Scottish steers – huge beasts with threatening horns, the tips of which surely would be lethal weapons should these prehistoric looking animals emerge from their complacency and leap the low stone walls that pen them in. Rather than endless extravagant mansions peeping out from enormous hedges, the Berkshires shows a mishmash of small, unpretentious houses, large tracts of open land, and occasionally the eye-filling view of a magnificent home once owned by some landed gentry a century ago. I get the feeling of retreating to another time and place, simple by today's standards, as people buy what they need at small retail establishments still owned by local residents. Music and theater are not performed in grand venues but often in barns or outdoor arenas. Interesting that I am looking to a new future by thinking of going to a place that seems to exist in the past.

January 15, 1991

After living the country club life for so many years, I can't believe that we are going to the Berkshires to rent a summer place. Joel and I have agreed to remain club members and try something new at the same time. This may incur quite a bit of expense, but we don't want to leave the club unless we are sure that we will be happy in our new environment.

We are used to a busy suburban lifestyle. The country will be quite a change. From our previous trips to Lenox, we have found life there to be slow paced, while we are used to charging around always in a hurry. There are few places to shop, while we are used to having a big mall just five minutes away. We walk to the adjacent small town of Westfield along tree-lined streets with lovely homes. In town are a dozen different outdoor restaurants. In the country we will be prepared to hike rather than walk, but we will see beautiful woods lined with old stone walls meandering past streams with mountains in the background. A rental is definitely the best way to feel out this possible change.

We invited Ellie and Jimmy Bowen to join us for the weekend, and their enthusiasm was rewarding. I have known Ellie since she was in graduate school. We met at a mutual friend's dinner party. My work as a high school counselor and social worker was exactly suited to her needs for a supervised internship for her graduation requirements. I was happy to take Ellie on as my intern. We worked together on a daily basis for six months. After all that togetherness only one of two things can happen: Two people either can't stand each other for another minute, or a warm and enduring friendship develops. What a moment of good luck – to have been at that dinner party and met Ellie, who continues to be a terrific addition to my life. She is delightful and easy going. She smiles readily, and, true to her calling as a guidance counselor, she always tries to make a situation comfortable for everyone. Jimmy has a wonderful sense of humor and has fun wherever he is. Joel and I will not have to worry that they will get bored or annoyed with the time we need to spend finding our rental, especially since Jimmy already seems to have his eye on which weekend he wants to come up.

The four of us checked our calendars and decided to spend the weekend of February 10th in the country. My friend and real estate broker Charlotte Gross has arranged to have us meet with a rental agent. I am so excited.

I have looked at a million guidebooks to the Berkshires but don't want to spend a million dollars over the weekend. I finally settled on a bed and breakfast in Lenox. Bedrooms with fireplaces and antique furniture sound like a fantasy to me. I picture a big dining room table with several other guests having convivial conversation while we help ourselves to the sideboard loaded with warm muffins, local honey, and fresh-squeezed juices. I see big flakes of snow falling quietly but persistently so that soon there is a fluffy white layer coating the town.

Sounds so good. I hope that the realization is as great as the anticipation.

February 10, 1991

I told our children about our decision to rent a home in the country. It seems that even grown children have misgivings about their parents making changes in their lives. "You're not going to be around this summer?" asked Mark, as if at age twenty-three he is not off with his friends whenever we would like to spend time with him. "The house will look so lonely without you there," said Nancy. My interpretation of that comment is, "Who will look after Danielle if we want to go out alone?" David and his wife Mindy also had plenty to say. "Do you realize what kind of traffic you will be fighting every weekend?" offered Mindy. "Not to mention the dangers of constantly being on the road," David added with a worried expression on his face. This really tickled me since I have had a countless sleepless nights worrying about David as he indulged in his passion for motorcycles. When did our kids begin to think they were our parents?

I explained to our children that this change is not all that dramatic. We had no intention of pulling up stakes to explore the Yukon. We were not looking to settle in the unspoiled parts of Colorado or Arizona. We were not even thinking of flying off to Florida. No, for us, change meant a rental for the summer months, slightly less than three hours from our home in north central New Jersey.

This morning, in spite our children's misgivings and the bitter February weather, Joel and I headed north. With adventurous spirits and with the company of Ellie and Jimmy, we were on our way to the Berkshire Hills of western Massachusetts.

We arrived in the old New England town of Lenox at around 12:30 and headed to the bed and breakfast I had booked for us. We were well rewarded with our choice. A big stone fireplace was ablaze with crackling logs, and a pot of steaming hot soup was set out on a large sideboard in the parlor. The hall was lined with Norman Rockwell prints. Laura and Jeff, the owners of the inn, greeted us with such extraordinary enthusiasm that I began to wonder if we were their only guests. It was possible that perhaps we had lost our sanity to be in Lenox in such inhospitable weather. The wind was so biting that even the most avid skier would be driven inside. Laura kindly offered us some of that wonderful New England clam chowder to take the chill off our bones and the edge off our appetites. Finally, we were eager to see our rooms, drop our things, and set out to wander around Lenox.

After the lovely greeting in those fabulous public rooms, we were taken to our accommodations. What a disappointment. The guidebook seductively described the inn as filled with vintage furniture and possessing old-world charm. I found that "vintage" just means old and musty. Musty rooms with old musty floral wallpaper and curtains. "Old-world charm" means uneven heat, cold floors, rusty bathtubs, and clanging pipes. My expectations of exquisite rooms with crisp linens and fluffy down quilts immediately vanished. As I gazed at the unappealing hobnail bedspreads and this room no bigger than a walk-in closet, I folded up those expectations and put them away for another time. This was to be our fantasy space for the next two days.

I felt bad for us but especially sorry for Ellie and Jimmy. Good sports, they assured me that this B&B was fine and we would all laugh about it at some other time. We telephoned the realtor Charlotte had recommended and made arrangements to meet her late in the afternoon, then we then set out to explore the town.

Quaint and unhurried, Lenox beckoned and did not disappoint. We were enchanted with small wonderful shops, one shelved with beautiful gifts, another tempting us to buy warm soft fleece-lined gloves, yet another with table settings of antique dishes and crystal stemware. Ellie and I stopped for a moment to imagine which Berkshire "cottage" had housed this tableware. My idea of a cottage is a small house with cozy rooms that envelope me in solitude and quiet. The Berkshire cottages are something else entirely. Grand old mansions with high ceilings, a multitude of enormous rooms, and space for a dozen live-in servants constitute what is curiously referred to as a cottage.

While Ellie and I were musing about what life around a dining room table would have been like in such a cottage, our husbands had found their own destination. Joel, a prolific reader, had no doubt about what he wanted to do. His instant fascination with the architecture of the Lenox Library lured him in like his favorite seven-layer cake in a bakery window. This Federal-style building is handsome and stately in its bearing, and the interior is as architecturally rewarding as its façade. When our shopping interests were satisfied, Ellie and I went to collect the guys at the library. There they were, looking like the lords of the manor sitting in oversized leather chairs surrounded by stacks of books. All they needed were glasses of sherry to complete the picture.

Our husbands' literary pleasure aside, at that point I needed food. I was suddenly beyond the hunger-pang stage into the hunger-fang stage. I was getting cranky, and when Joel sees that personality change, he knows that my fangs are coming down. So it was with the knowledge that I was close to taking a bite out of his neck that we hastily entered the first restaurant we saw. What a lucky find – a café whose snow-laden porch implied a time of year when patrons took their lunch under a warm summer sun. With 18 degrees on the thermometer, we were comforted to be seated inside at a window table overlooking Church Street. Warmed by the hot mulled cider, we relaxed and ordered a hearty lunch of perfectly grilled burgers served on thick crusty French bread. After warm apple tart and steaming coffee, we were ready to meet our realtor in the nearby town of Stockbridge, five miles south of Lenox.

I instantly fell in love with picturesque Stockbridge, and the rest of our group agreed that this is as close to small-town heaven as it gets.

We entered the Main Street office of Wheeler and Taylor Realtors and Insurers, and introduced ourselves to Sally, whom we found to be knowledgeable and helpful. Charmingly eccentric in demeanor, she reminded me of Julia Child, with that familiar expressive voice, tilt of her head, and slightly hesitant manner. I find her quite endearing, and I was comfortable working with her.

We told her were looking to rent a house, not a condo, from Memorial Day through Labor Day. It would be nice to have four bedrooms, I proposed. Immediately, Jimmy chimed in that he would like to have a room with an attached bath. That sounded like big trouble to me. Ignoring Jimmy, Joel proceeded to mention that it was important for us to be close to Tanglewood. This area is the summer home of the Boston Symphony Orchestra and our love of music, classical music especially, is the main reason we were drawn to the Berkshires to begin with. We also threw in a small glitch – our budget.

"Let me see what I can do for you," said Sally, her brow furrowed and her brain visibly engaged. She promised to call us first thing tomorrow morning and set us on our way to a season in the country. I hope. With that curious tilt of her head, she waved a goodbye.

When we left her office and approached the street to cross to our car, we noticed something unfamiliar. As we looked right and then left, all manner of traffic stopped to permit us safe passage in crossing the street. No! There was no police officer. No! There was no stop sign. No! There was no traffic light. There was simply a sign saying "Pedestrians Have the Right of Way." We shook our heads in delightful disbelief as we walked casually in front of an eighteen-wheel tractor-trailer heading east for Route 7, a tourist bus heading west towards Route 102, and a line of cars and SUVs in both directions on Main Street.

Courtesy of the The Red Lion Inn, Stockbridge, MA, ©Kristian Septimius Krogh

By this time I was hungry again. It was seven o'clock and time to eat. The Red Lion Inn is the calling card to Stockbridge. Built around 1773, it had been vanquished by fire in the late 1800s. It was fully rebuilt and served as a stop on the route to Boston for weary travelers looking for respite from the harsh terrain and ceaseless cold. Jack and Jane Fitzpatrick have faithfully maintained the quintessential New England inn since they purchased it in the 1960s. Charming rooms and scrumptious food continue to comfort lucky Berkshire visitors.

The steps to the huge wrap-around porch are flanked by two bronze lions. We approached the inn like the beacon of comfort it was on this frosty wind-whipped evening. Ellie and Jimmy had never been to the Red Lion, and I knew they would be drawn in by its true New England ambiance. The oversized fireplace was throwing off an abundance of heat. A huge crock of cheese surrounded by crackers and strawberries was set in the lobby for guests. It was a welcomed sight, as by this point even Ellie and Jimmy became a bit concerned when they saw that hungry look in my eye. With plates overflowing with hors d'oeuvres and glasses of red wine, we relaxed in front of the fireplace. I was satisfied and everyone was relieved. We entered the dining room about half an hour later and ordered the best turkey dinner this side of Thanksgiving. Talk about comfort food. Wonderful mashed potatoes, homemade cranberry sauce, piles of turkey on piles of stuffing, all followed by bread pudding for dessert. Stuffed and happy we returned to Lenox.

Joel and I said good night to the Bowens and found ourselves snug – very snug – in our small room with vintage furniture and old-world charm.

We have had plenty of snow this winter in New Jersey, but somehow it always looks black from the spewing of automobile exhaust. Here, it seems that the snow stays brilliantly white. We also live in a small picturesque town, but trying to cross the street after the policeman goes off duty is a risk that I am never willing to take. Here it seems that crossing the street is part of a calm and civilized way of life.

I am so sleepy that I wonder if all this serenity is more of a dream than a reality. We'll see tomorrow.

February 11, 1991

Breakfast was included in the price of our rooms, and at eight o'clock this morning the smell of the freshest coffee floated up the staircase. The familiar perfume of muffins just ready to be pulled from the oven had our noses twitching with anticipation. These fragrances were urging Joel and me to dress quickly and hurry down to the dining room to satisfy our gastronomical lust.

This was not as easy at it should have been. After bumping into each other two or three times, the size of the room began to get on our nerves. I couldn't find my snow boots, which had been kicked under the bed when Joel needed to get up in the middle of the night. Joel couldn't find his hat, which was crushed under a pile of yesterday's clothes. I didn't really care about his flattened hat, and by this time he didn't give a hoot if my feet froze and fell off my legs. "Stop yelling, everyone will hear us," I said softly. At this point we saw the silliness of it all, and with a laugh we left our room. We didn't really have to worry about "everyone" because it turned that I was right – we were the only guests in the inn. When we reached the dining room, no one was there but Ellie and Jimmy. Those just-from-the-oven muffins, an array of cereals, and hardboiled eggs joined pots of coffee and hot chocolate on the sideboard. Our host and hostess were gracious and hospitable. They gave us bits of advice and information on the Berkshires, and informed us that they themselves had come to Lenox from a large metropolitan area to find a quieter life.

After breakfast we headed once again to Wheeler and Taylor, this time to the Great Barrington office. Sally was obviously set to go as she greeted us at the door. Six hours and a dozen houses later, we had settled on a 180-year-old Federal-style house located just minutes from Tanglewood. "Our" house is well situated on a main road in Stockbridge, about halfway between the towns of Great Barrington and Lenox. Most importantly, one of the bedrooms is set up as a nursery. The crib did it. A room all ready for baby Danielle.

Joel and I made the commitment. With three other bedrooms, a modernized kitchen, and plenty of room at the antique farm table for friends and family, the house is just perfect. It has wide planked pine floors, deep sofas and chairs, and a real wood-burning stove, which adds lots of character to the living room. Jimmy did wince a little at the idea of one bathroom servicing the four bedrooms, but he had the good sense not to express himself out loud. Pleased and exhausted, we again parted company with Sally and headed back to the inn for a rest.

Evening found us ravenously hungry – what a shock! Ellie and Jimmy have old friends in the area, and so the four of us joined the four of them for an evening of great fun and good food. In this way we met the Osbornes and the Shepherds, the first – I hope – of many new friends to come.

Too soon, our weekend ended. Why is it that everything fits into the suitcase when we are going someplace, but there seems to be no room for the very same stuff when I repack to go home? We did finally coerce all our belongings back into the cases and loaded the car. Lying through our teeth, we told Laura and Jeff how much we enjoyed staying at the inn. The vintage furniture and old-world charm would always have a place in our memory. They were both so delighted they kissed us all goodbye. And that will be the last they ever see of us.

We have much to look forward to. The snow and bracing cold will be a distant and fond memory when next we see the Berkshire Hills. Will this be the new beginning I have been looking for? Suddenly the future is before us once again.

May 12, 1991

This was the first day in our Berkshires rental house. I woke up to the smells of the country – the fragrances of hay and cut grass – and the olfactory awareness of cows from a nearby farm. The O'Gradys, who own the house, have been so gracious. Encouraging us to have guests and leaving a bottle of champagne for us to toast our new adventure, they have made us feel that this is our home. They even told us to use their canoe, which is housed in the garage. I can't believe we have rented this wonderful place for the next three-and-a-half months.

With all their earlier resistance, our kids are now asking how often they can come up or, better yet, when we will be in New Jersey so that they can bring their friends and have the house to themselves.

Jimmy and Ellie Bowen have their weekend picked out, and Jimmy did not even crack a joke about how he expects to meet us in the middle of the night as we head to the one bathroom. Joel and I are delighted to have them as our first guests; after all they went through with us last winter, they are entitled to enjoy the spoils.

Today we purchased an inexpensive bistro table and chairs so we can enjoy breakfast on the small patio outside the kitchen door. A pretty green and white umbrella completed the setting. Our walk around "the estate" this morning revealed the inlet to the Stockbridge Bowl. How fabulous to take the canoe and just drop it into the lake.

Joel even has a golf game, which came in a somewhat roundabout fashion. This past February, we had that agreeable dinner with the Osborns and the Shepherds, friends of the Bowens. Recently Joe Osborn called Joel to ask if he was available to play in a tournament at the Stockbridge Golf Club. Joel was enthusiastic in his response and then Joe told him that his friend Ralph Gomberg was looking for a partner for the upcoming Trophy Tournament. Joel agreed to partner up with Ralph, even though they had never met. It amazes me that Joel has no qualms about spending two full days playing golf with someone he doesn't know. I have to admire him, for I would be much more skeptical.

July 21, 1991

This was the weekend of the Trophy Tournament. Friday, Ralph Gomberg came by to pick up Joel for a practice round. It was instant affection between the two of them. Ralph bounded up the steps to the house, kissing me hello and solidly shaking Joel's hand. He was ready to play. His sense of anticipation was heightened by the fact that Joel is a 5 handicap golfer and Ralph, an 18, was already thinking about the possibility of a win.

Up here in the Berkshires, tournaments are played in flights. The first round on Saturday placed the teams in flight according to their score. Joel and Ralph were in the sixth flight. Saturday evening the club had a dinner for the players and spouses, and Joel and I met Ralph's wife Sydelle. It was then that we discovered that Ralph was the retired principal oboist of the Boston Symphony and Sydelle was the retired director of the Boston Ballet School. We gladly shared information about our children and grandchildren, and felt so very relaxed with one another.

Sure enough, Ralph was a happy guy today, as he and Joel easily won their flight.

This evening Ralph asked us if we would like to join the Stockbridge Golf Club. We both leaped at the invitation, and we now have Ralph ready to sponsor us into the club. Mother is appalled that we will belong to two golf clubs. I have explained to her that we are incurring a very modest expense in joining the Stockbridge Club and that eventually we may drop out of one place or another depending upon the way our lives take shape. So far, this Berkshire life seems to be just what we had been looking for. Ironic that many years ago belonging to one country club seemed a preposterous idea and now I am ready to belong to two clubs.

September 2, 1991

Labor Day Weekend has arrived. Wow, the summer went fast. We had fabulous nights at Tanglewood, leisurely picnics on the big farm table under the trees in the yard, and so much fun paddling the canoe in the Stockbridge Bowl.

As luxurious as it was, though, there were times when having two lifestyles, one in New Jersey and the other in the Berkshires, created tensions we hadn't expected. As each weekend approached we often felt the two environments tugging at us. Do we miss the weekend in the country to attend someone's birthday party? Should we play in the tournament at Shackamaxon or the tournament at the Stockbridge club? What about our theater subscription in New York? What do we do about those tickets for Saturday? Give them away, sell them, or stay and go into the city? It makes we wonder how the really rich and famous manage all their toys. I guess Mother is right when she tells me that these are "champagne" problems. I don't know where she came up with a line like that, but it seems so perfect when I create a dilemma out of silly, almost meaningless issues. The phrase always reminds me of how lucky we are, sometimes, to have nothing more serious than champagne problems to solve.

We have already told the O'Gradys that we would like to return next summer. This adventure has surely been a success and now the supreme luxury – which is to pack our things, lock the door, and have no Berkshire-house worries all through the fall, winter, and spring.

July 18, 1997

After finishing the old diary this evening, I realized that I hadn't written a word for the five years between renting the O'Grady house and my current journal, which chronicles life from that fateful decision to buy our own home. This latest journal is always on my desk. It stares at me each evening until a great guilt overcomes me and I finally begin to fill its pages once more. As I thought about writing my next entry, I was drawn to page one, and instead of writing I began to read once more.

Part Two

April 17, 1996

Our friend and realtor Charlotte Gross has been crisscrossing the Berkshire countryside trying to find the perfect setting for our second and more permanent commitment. We have spent five wonderful years in our Stockbridge rental house. Our growing family has begun to strain under the discomfort of one bathroom and no air conditioning. Grandchildren fill the space with toys and a palpable energy that, after a two-day visit, begins to manifest itself in frayed nerves and tempers just about to erupt from under polite exteriors. While Charlotte is doing her best to help us become homeowners instead of seasonal renters, Joel and I have been engaging in our own mental crisscrossing about whether or not we actually need a second home. The cons have given way to the pros, and we have finally decided to start a search for our dream house. Of course, Mother thinks we've lost our minds and is sure that this venture will land us in what she refers to as "the poor house."

It is not unusual for Joel and me to come at ideas from different points of view, and while we both agree that we want a home of our own, we have different needs. I cling to the wish to be close to Tanglewood, and Joel longs for mountain views. Charlotte has taken us to see endless properties – some promising but perhaps too far from Lenox, others not so promising but with fabulous expansive views. The hunt has been ongoing, and yesterday we asked to see a house that has been piquing our interest because it has both location and views. It has taken us a while to summon the courage to inspect this house, as it resembles nothing even close to what we think of as a New England hideaway. We'd had dreams of old Federal-style houses or shingled homes with welcoming wraparound porches. This one, however, is an exact replica of a tract house from a New Jersey bedroom community. Charlotte shook her head in disbelief, but she did as we asked and arranged entry into the house.

This afternoon we met the listing broker in the driveway and after fumbling with the key for a few minutes he finally opened the front door.

"Tract house motif" was not what I was looking for, let alone a dwelling so dark and brooding as to be entirely inhospitable. The entry way was immediately off-putting. Shag carpet covered the hall and family room, and floral carpet covered the rest of the floors except for the kitchen, which boasted a deep mustard linoleum. I looked hopelessly on old cabinets with doors that didn't quite close and appliances encrusted with the layered scum of an old oil tank. Nothing, to that point, made me want to buy this house. With weary determination to be a good sport, I followed everyone up the narrow staircase, a musty odor – redolent of perhaps a decaying mouse – in the air. We walked from room to room, I sinking deeper and deeper into myself and Joel gamely asking questions about this or that as if we could possibly see ourselves living here.

It was in one of the bedrooms, all of them having tiny windows and oddly themed wallpaper, that a voice filled with panic rose up from my throat. "I have to get out of here," I declared. "Now! This second! I think I'm having an attack of claustrophobia." Out I walked, leaving two stunned brokers and my husband paying no attention to me but marveling over the vast mountain views that were barely visible from the tiny windows.

Wandering around the perimeter of the house was not much help. An above-ground pool set in a dark brown crumbling deck. The yard, a mess with trees and bushes so overgrown that they seemed to be marching toward the house itself, as Hamlet's Burnham Wood advanced towards Dunsinane Castle.

True to Joel's desires, the house had great views, and true to my desires, the house was near Tanglewood – but NO, a thousand times no. I will not buy a tract house with an attached two-car garage and plastic grills in the windows. No plastic grills for me. I want authenticity, character, history. This house is definitely not what I'm looking for. I am certain of that. I am exhausted. Got to sleep now.

December 9, 1996

Joel and I battled about the house for a week. He thought it was fabulous and I thought it was the reincarnation of the Bates Motel from that old Hitchcock movie. We went back and forth, each of us trying to convince the other about the positives or negatives of this miserably unpleasant property.

So we closed on the house in July.

After spending the summer and fall in the rental house, we are now in our newly renovated home. This process of renovating had, at its core, what I call the three ex's: exhilarating, exhausting, and expensive. There are times when Joel and I seem to be amazingly incompatible. As a matter of fact, I can't imagine two people more opposite in disposition and behavior. We do share a common view of what makes us comfortable though, and when I finally became resigned to the fact that this, believe it or not, was going to be our new home, we discovered that architectural change was going to come easy.

The sculptor tells us that a piece of marble speaks to him, encouraging his chisel to chip away here and smooth out there until the stone itself has the honor of the creation, leaving the sculptor merely the mechanical instrument of the stone's final incarnation. As with the marble, our homely excuse of a country house told us firmly what to do. We simply became its tool.

"Gut me," it said. *"Spend huge quantities of money,"* it roared. *"Take out one of the bedrooms on the second floor creating a two-story hall for light and air. Remove the entire back wall and put in large double-hung windows and French doors, so the endless mountain views become the focus. Add a bathroom to each existing bedroom, so Jimmy can be comfortable when he visits."*

The house spoke to us again and again. *"Remove the dark paneling in the den and turn it into a guest bedroom. Add old pine floors and change the staircase. Take the kitchen down to the studs and add the finest cabinets and state-of-the-art appliances. More, more, more!"* cried the tract house, obviously wanting to be transformed into a true Berkshire hideaway.

The house was ceaseless in its demands, and we were helpless and weak. "Yes," we kept saying to the house, even as we crept past our budget. "What else do you want, house?" we asked meekly. *"Build me a large two-story porch and spare no expense, for I need a structure that will not budge an inch when confronted with a nor'easter that could dump four feet of snow on my second-story planked porch floor. And don't forget columns. I want big round columns to support this two-level porch. Maybe fluted columns, ones that would be worthy of a fine Southern plantation."*

Well, I do believe it was the request for columns that finally shook us back to reality. By this time we had soared past our budget with the swiftness of a rocket blasting through earth's atmosphere, speeding faster and faster out of control. We had to put on the breaks and stop the flow of money demanded by our newly transformed country home. While we find ourselves with what is arguably the most extraordinary second-story porch floor in all of western Massachusetts, alas, our columns are no more than ordinary 4 x 4 support posts.

Friends are amazed at the speed with which our project has been completed. In six weeks, ninety percent of the work was accomplished. Arthur, our architect, had never seen a renovation as complex as this completed at such an incredible pace. It did help to have David in the construction business. Our son's fabulous crew came up from New Jersey and just worked ceaselessly until the house was pretty close to finished. The crew worked so fast that Arthur would draw up plans in the morning that the men would execute in the afternoon. With the added cooperation of local experts in heating and air conditioning, as well as plumbers and electricians who miraculously appeared from Pittsfield or Lee on what seemed to be a moment's notice, we are now comfortably set to have our first guests in our own Berkshire home.

The last ten percent of the work, involving some interior painting and exterior siding, is now being done by a fellow recommended to us by friends. Stanley always shows up on time, exactly a day later than he promised. He is firm on his prices, until we get bills for work he decided was more involved than he originally estimated. He has designed and built shelves framing the fireplace. Stanley does beautiful work, but not the first time. There always needs to be a second fabrication before things fit the way they should. Stanley works neatly, but only after I hand him a vacuum and a broom. He has yet to complete those myriad details that take a house from the stage called livable to that imaginary state called "finished." Will that ever happen? Who knows?

So, this morning, in spite of the shivering chill in the air, I went out on our wrap-around porch with a cup of coffee and surveyed all we had done. The house is wonderful, but the project tested the fabric of our marriage. Our surviving intact, from the initial viewing through the process of reinventing this ugly tract house, had its shaky moments. As I sat on the porch, hands cupping my hot coffee and a warm fleece robe drawn tightly around my waist, it all seemed to come together. They say the broken leg, when healed, is stronger than ever – as it is with me and Joel. I think this adventure has made us stronger. I am finally contented. The family will come for the holidays. Our children, grandchildren, and my parents will no doubt "ooh" and "aah" with delight and only I will notice that the banister needs another coat of stain, that the slider to the porch doesn't glide as easily as it should and that the tile in front of the fireplace needs to be re-grouted. But as Mother would say, "These are just champagne problems, darling." And I know she will be right.

April 3, 1997

I spent all winter and spring finishing up the house. How fabulous to see the transformation from that ugly white elephant into a home that invites me and Joel each weekend with the promise of tranquility and comfort. The furnishings are a mix of old and new pieces. A rare handmade wormy chestnut dining table found its way from our New Jersey basement to Stockbridge, along with six ladder-back chairs painted blue with a distressed finish that has a wonderful country look. A wrought iron fixture over the table bathes the room in real candlelight, casting changing shadows on the ceiling as the darkness outside deepens from dusk to night. We bought area rugs from catalogues in hues of yellow and blue, and purchased inexpensive white slipcover couches to be placed at right angles in front of the fireplace. We've decided to have both a winter and a summer décor. Next winter our blue and yellow rugs will be rolled up and replaced by ruby red Orientals. I had pillows made in a red tartan plaid and found red tartan lampshades to cover the hall chandelier. Joel and I found a local artist to do a painting depicting various aspects of Stockbridge in summer's splendor. She included the bell tower, whose chimes each evening at six o'clock remind golfers on the eighteenth hole that the day is coming to an end. She added the Red Lion Inn and the ever-flowing Housatonic River as well as the Berkshire Hills so visible from our house. We have this painting over the fireplace and have asked the artist to paint a similar version with the town splendid in winter white. I think it will be so much fun to run around each fall and spring changing the feel and the look of the house. (On second thought, I can just hear Joel getting irritated as I ask him for the fourth time to help me roll up the winter rugs and roll out the summer rugs.)

A trip to Macy's in Albany turned out to be worth the hour's ride. A huge clearance sale was in place, and we purchased three bedroom sets. Along with Nancy's old pine bed, our place is nearly complete. It is so much fun wandering around Marshalls and K-Mart picking up an inexpensive pitcher or a table runner hidden in the clearance aisle. I would much rather dress up my house than dress up myself. The size of my closet attests to the fact that I have no interest in clothes shopping. Instead, I have clearly become obsessed with making sure that even the tiniest detail in our house is attended to.

Joel worries that I am losing my mind as I go from store to store, aisle to aisle, looking for the perfect soap dish for each bathroom. Each bedroom must have the most exquisite antique candy dish, for our guests might need a chocolate fix in the middle of the night as they get up to use the bathroom. I filled old wicker baskets with magazines from *Architectural Digest* to *Zoos of the Berkshires* and rolled and tied them with beautiful ribbons – after all, our guests probably need something to read as well as chocolates to eat in the middle of the night. Certainly, friends might get thirsty while they are reading and eating chocolates after they go to the bathroom in the middle of the night, in which case I have found unbelievably gorgeous stemmed etched glasses to place next to imported spring water. Joel has guaranteed me that, one Sunday night after the guests have left, I will find one of those irreplaceable stemmed glasses in at least two pieces. So what? For now, everything is just the way I want it. No one coming to our home will have the disappointed reaction I so clearly remember when we first arrived at that "charming old-world inn" in Lenox.

Now that the house is close to complete and visitors will be joining us soon, I am as excited as Cinderella going to the ball. We have turned our pumpkin of a dwelling into a golden coach, and I am proud to show it off. Our friends will surely appreciate the change from the old rental place, wonderful as it was, to our air-conditioned coach with a bathroom for each bedroom.

At the last minute, Sonny and Bob Kohn decided to ride up from New Jersey for a quick overnight. Joel and I were thrilled. After they called we went to stock up on some items for lunch, and when we returned, waiting for us on the front step was the most beautiful clay flower pot, overflowing with gorgeous ketchup-red geraniums. The pot was huge and added just the right touch of country charm to our entryway. We found Sonny and Bob sitting on the screened porch, and went out to greet them. Bob looked exhausted, so exhausted I momentarily forgot to thank them for their spectacular gift. He was perspiring and needed some water. "What's wrong?" I asked, really concerned. "You know that damn pot out front?" he gasped. "Sonny had me carry it here to the rear porch. Then she decided she didn't like it here, so I carried it out to the beginning of the driveway. She didn't like it there either, so next I carried it to the entry door, and now I think I'm getting a hernia."

Half an hour later, Bob felt much better although he was a bit hunched from his sore back. We finally could tell our guests how deeply we appreciated their fabulous gift. It meant so very much to us that they would go to such thought and trouble to launch our new home.

We had a wonderful day, and we made plans for Sonny and Bob to make a return trip later in the summer. That will be their official first visit. I hope by then Bob will be able to stand up straight.

July 23, 1997

Wow, it is finally Wednesday. I have passed the last four nights engrossed in the past. After finishing the first Stockbridge journal, I have spent time reading those entries that were written just last year. Now that I have reminded myself once again how I managed to be here at this time and place, it seems fitting to move on, thankful for tomorrow, Thursday, when Joel will return and I can feel the electricity of his presence. A moment I always welcome – the anticipated opening of the door as he comes back for another few days. I am committed, dear journal, to continuing to fill your pages, but, of course, only as the whim of the moment dictates.

August 6, 1997

Today was sheer fantasy. It was supposed to be a casual lunch so that Jane Kelner could meet an old acquaintance, my friend Lynda. It turned into one of those days I will not easily forget. Lynda and Jim arrived yesterday as did Bob and Sonny who joined us for the sixth year in a row. They have claimed the weekend of the Boston Symphony's Tanglewood on Parade as their time in our home. This event holds for them the sanctity of a holy pilgrimage, and we never tire of their company.

The six of us are a great group and usually keep tightly to ourselves. Jim, Bob, and I have not succeeded in keeping the liberal Democrat ladies and my arch-conservative husband from screaming at each other, but somehow or another we enjoy these sadomasochistic weekends more than the Marquis de Sade liked his leathers.

I had decided to have this lunch because Jane and Lynda hadn't seen each other since Jane moved out of New Jersey to the Berkshires five years ago. By the time I got through calling one friend after another, we were up to twenty-two guests. Then Joel called Ralph and Sydelle Gomberg and invited them as well. We were delighted to hear them accept, especially since Ralph has not been in the best of health.

As usual, I had to think carefully about the menu. We had the Atkins dieters and the people who cannot eat nuts, shellfish, or fat. OK. Overstuffed sandwiches filled with smoked Gouda, roasted red peppers, and sliced red onion would satisfy some. In addition, I made a huge Caesar salad with grilled chicken. Trays of assorted cheeses and bowls of fresh fruit rounded out the lunch. Our houseguests had brought plenty of white wine, and I knew we had a party in the making.

Breakfast came and went, and everything was going smoothly for our lunch. Lynda and Sonny set the tables. We decided to have hors d'oeuvres on the patio and then luncheon in the living/dining room. Bob split the baguettes we had bought at the Daily Bread Bakery. He thinly sliced the

Gouda cheese while I was grilling the chicken on the stove. All seemed right with the world.

Suddenly we heard Jim yelling from the basement. "What's wrong?" I screamed back in a panic. "The basement is flooded" was the reply. "I think I know where the leak is coming from, but I'm not sure I can fix it." Since Joel needs an electrician to fix a light bulb and I am not much better, I knew we didn't even have a screwdriver. "What do you think you need?" I asked as I walked into the basement and saw, to my horror, Jim standing in two feet of water and plugging up the leak with his finger. "I've got the leak. It's coming from the humidifier, but I need a wrench to turn the knob that shuts off the water."

Who to call? I new I couldn't reach my plumber in the middle of the morning. It would not do to keep Jim plugging up the leak for the rest of the weekend – Joel and I do try hard to keep our guests happy and comfortable. It dawned on me that our neighbor Alan was as handy as we are unhandy. A quick phone call, and Alan came to the rescue with his toolbox. Jim found the wrench he needed and turned off the offending valve. Although the basement now needs to be water vacuumed, disaster was averted. With our problem staved off until winter, when we will actually need a humidifier, the plans for lunch continued. And what a lunch it was.

Today was a true August day. Blazing sun, hot temperatures, and not a breeze moving a leaf from its place on the tree. In spite of this, I had decided to go ahead with drinks outside under the canopy. As if they had had some prior discussion, all our guests arrived at once. We enjoyed our iced drinks and veggies and dip and each other. Not long after, to everyone's relief we went inside – so wonderfully cool by comparison. We had set up two tables and everyone quickly found their name cards. I had taken time with the seating arrangements, as I wanted each group to be interesting and diverse, but I had not foreseen that the day would wind up with everyone gathered together.

Our guests attacked the sideboard with gusto, filling their plates so high that soon I was back in the kitchen making extra sandwiches. I could hear a constant chatter in the room, sometimes interrupted by thunderous laughter from one table or another. Ralph and Sydelle were at the head of the large dining room table. We have loved Ralph since that first meeting in the old rental house. When I returned with more food, I noticed that Ralph was somewhat reserved. I wanted so much for him to get pleasure from this day. His sense of humor was always acute, but today, apparently feeling less than vigorous, he played the part of a listener and not a participant. Joel and the kids often accuse me of managing every situation, but isn't that part of my job description – seeing to it that all goes as well as possible? I dug deep into myself to bring up the most effective of managerial skills, determined somehow to manage to get Ralph more fully engaged in the conversation. "Ralph," I said rather loudly, so all would pay attention, "why don't you share some of your stories about life in the symphony? Would you tell everyone how you eventually got to the Boston Symphony in the first place?" The manager did it again. Ralph looked up from his plate and nodded to indicate a willingness to comply with my request. As he started to speak, a faint sparkle replaced the glaze that had previously shadowed his eyes. Everyone stopped chewing. The clang of forks and knives colliding with china ceased. Each one of us in that room has reverence for the Symphony, and to have such a distinguished member of the Orchestra as Ralph ready to share some bits of his life was a little like traveling with Dorothy down the yellow brick road. The room was quiet and the group at the other table began to amble over with their chairs. One of those guests was George Minkoff, a rare book dealer and archivist of much note.

Ralph recounted his entry into the Boston Symphony Orchestra. He had been living in California as a young man. He had a friend, also an accomplished musician, living there as well. Both he and the friend were not having much luck gaining the positions they were seeking in the music world, so they had come to Hollywood to play background for the movies. One day the friend approached Ralph with an opportunity to join him in the building business. Ralph weighed the possibilities. Returning to New York would allow him to pursue his relationship with a beautiful young ballet dancer. He would also take this opportunity to pursue once again a career in his chosen field. He called his old friend

Leonard Bernstein, who was conductor of the New York Symphony. "Lenny," he said, "do you have a place for me with the orchestra?" "This is your lucky day, Ralph. We happen to need you" was Bernstein's response. Ralph caught the next plane to New York City and joined Bernstein, eventually following him to Boston. This is how Ralph Gomberg came to enjoy his lasting tenure with the BSO and a long adoring relationship with the lovely Sydelle. He contends to this day that, although his friend in California became very wealthy in the building business, the wealth Ralph derived from his life in the Symphony is unmatched.

Coincidently, George was the archivist for the Bernstein papers. And from there, the afternoon was off to George and Ralph trading "Lenny" stories, one after the other. I surprised everyone by telling my own Lenny story.

A few years ago, Joel and I decided to collect autographs of famous people. We bought a book on autograph collecting and then made our first purchase – a paper signed by Albert Einstein. We found out that the worth of an autograph increases depending on several factors: first, the signature; second, a dated signature; third, a personal letter; and so on, each factor contributing to the value of the acquisition. One Sunday a number of years ago, Joel and I were lucky enough to sneak into a closed rehearsal in the Shed at Tanglewood. Bernstein was rehearsing the orchestra, and only two or three other people were in the audience. Joel suggested that I grab a program from the floor and ask Bernstein for an autograph. I was feeling a little intimidated, but when the rehearsal was over, I decided to go for it. I followed a man up to the stage who secured Bernstein's autograph first. Then it was my turn. The Maestro graciously autographed my program, but when I looked down at the signature, I was mildly disappointed as it was not dated. I innocently looked up into his eyes and said, "How about a date?" I knew what I meant, so I was completely startled when Bernstein took my face in his hands and said to me, "You are adorable," and walked off the stage. Still on the stage, I looked down at Joel, who was gleefully laughing while I was completely confused. "What happened?" I asked. "You dummy," he said, "he thought you were asking him to go on a date." We still laugh over this, and today was no exception.

What began as a pleasant idea for lunch and almost ended with a disastrous flood, turned into one of the most enchanting afternoons. It was uplifting for all, especially for Ralph, who came in rather pale and frail and left with a sprightly gait and a bloom on his face.

Our lunch was over, but the day had more to come. Jim and Lynda hung back with us. Napping was a priority after our hectic morning and lunch. Sonny and Bob left for Tanglewood on Parade at 2:30. They enjoy the entire day's activities while Joel and I are happy to get up there in time for our picnic dinner and the 8:30 concert, despite how much we love Tanglewood. The summer home of the Boston Symphony is the mainstay of the Berkshires. In our minds it has given the area its worldwide recognition. There is such magic at Tanglewood. It is lush and verdant with acres of manicured lawns anchored by giant trees whose gnarled roots spread far beyond their trunks, their canopy of leaves benevolently shielding us from the beating August sun. This place that feels inhabited by the ghosts of brilliant musicians and conductors of years past still opens its gates and welcomes the elite of the world's greatest talents. Serge Koussevitzky, the first conductor to bring the BSO to Tanglewood over half a century ago, set a standard of excellence that has not been compromised to this day by those who succeeded him, such as Charles Munch, Leonard Bernstein, and currently the magnetic Seji Ozawa.

From the last week in June through the end of August, Tanglewood is alive with every kind of musical experience. The classical Symphony holds sway on most evenings, but at other times Joel and I are enthralled by Keith Lockhart and the Boston Pops, with the songs of such regulars as James Taylor or the world's great jazz artists entertaining us each year over Labor Day weekend.

Some lazy Saturdays, with the scent of wet grass still lingering from the early morning dew, I sit on the great lawn with a book and a crunchy croissant listening to the rehearsal of the Sunday concert. On any ordinary weeknight we have frequently popped up to Tanglewood to listen to the Music Center students work on their material.

Thursdays, I often ride my bike to listen to the "Walks and Talks." I meet Charlotte Gross, Marilyn Kraft, and Sheila Dorn. We take our bagged lunches into the tent, chat with each other, and munch soggy sandwiches until our attention is called to the podium. We are then treated to the lectures of Tanglewood's famous guest soloists or composers. We might listen to one of the symphony musicians speaking about the complexities of playing in a large orchestra. He or she might tell us what life is like on the road or about the adjustment that needs to be made to a new conductor. Soft breezes, good company, and fascinating speakers – this is how any old Thursday in the summer has become a weekly standout. As the afternoon concludes and I ride my bike back home, the views of the Stockbridge Bowl and surrounding Berkshire Hills seem new once again. None of us takes for granted that we are privileged to share in this extraordinary experience called Tanglewood.

Meantime, after the luncheon Sonny and Bob took their chairs, which they leave with us all year as insurance that they will return, and headed to Tanglewood this hot Tuesday in August. Tanglewood on Parade is an all-day event which showcases the many segments that make up the Tanglewood summer season. Performances by the Boston Pops, the Boston Symphony, the Tanglewood Chorus, the Tanglewood Music Center, and the Boston University Tanglewood Institute for high school students take place from two o'clock in the afternoon through the gala evening concert.

It was, as usual, a spectacular evening. The Shed was sold out weeks in advance and the lawn was packed with families and friends setting out picnics worthy of kings and queens from foreign lands. They came laden with tables, beautiful linens, candelabras, and good china. Hampers filled with fancy foods and expensive wines added to the air of festivity. We did a much simpler picnic. Sandwiches, paper plates (although pretty ones), some cold summer wine. Joel, Bob, Lynda, and Jim were set to spend the evening on the lawn. Sonny and I prefer to be inside as close as possible to the stage, and we had the good fortune to get last-minute tickets in the very center of the first row. All seemed peaceful and gentle, as if we were in some kind of time warp.

Courtesy of The Boston Symphony Orchestra, Boston, MA, ©Stu Rosner

But there came a moment that evening when the unthinkable happened. People left their belongings only to return and find that others had moved their chairs and blankets. The lawn was so crowded that space was at a premium. The time warp was unfortunately lifted, and life as we know it intruded quickly. Epithets were flying, accusations abounded, the territorial law of the jungle was out there. Each situation eventually resolved itself, if not to everyone's satisfaction. Agitation and annoyance had replaced the splendid feeling of wellbeing on that small parcel of earth earlier in the day. An aura of "let's make the best of what is left of the day" prevailed. Then the music began and lifted us once more.

The concert was fantastic, ending as it always does with a blaring rendition of the 1812 Overture led by Ozawa, his arms flailing, his shoulder-length mane of grey hair moving, swirling almost in rhythm to the sound of his heavy breathing – a sound so deep and mystical that those of us in the first few rows become swept away, captured in some momentary space that lies beyond the wooden seats and metal posts of this plain utilitarian shed. Behind us in the darkness we could hear the Civil War–era cannons splitting the air with booms of rapid fire at the appropriate time in the music. Maestro Ozawa looked towards the back of the Shed as if his very gaze were powerful enough to bring forth each boom of the cannon. Though we have heard this same piece for many years, it remains remarkably new and exciting. One firing after another, boom, boom, and each time we allow it to shock, even when we know what to expect. It is as if we are complicit with the orchestra, the conductor, and the cannons in that we refuse to be jaded by its yearly repetitions.

The drama continued as the fireworks that concluded the evening shimmered over the Stockbridge Bowl outshining the brightest lights in the sky. More booms, these accompanied by shooting stars falling to earth and rockets screeching towards the heavens. There were squeals of pleasure and cries of fright from one or two small children. Fifteen minutes later, a silence fell on Tanglewood, signaling the time when all those fantastic picnic set-ups were to be dismantled and carried back to cars in distant parking lots. Thousands of us quietly leaving for our homes carrying our chairs, leftover programs, and blankets. It is always one of those moments of awesome quiet. I was overcome with gratitude for the fates that gave me life in this great land. Then, breaking the spell, Bob said, "How about some ice cream?" That's how we ended Tanglewood on Parade.

Good night, dear journal.

August 17, 1997

Most of our guests have been part of our lives for a long time. A few are old school chums. There are couples we met as newlyweds and whose friendships we still cherish. To this list we have added, over the years, people like Ellie Bowen from work environments, others from our country club, and those we have met through friends and through friends of friends. Our ever expanding list of relationships has only enriched our lives and we are so happy to share our beautiful Berkshires with them. However, I am increasingly aware that time spent with friends around a set activity for a day at a time differs markedly from spending unstructured weekends together, especially since I seem to feel it is my responsibility to ensure that everyone has a fabulous time. After today, it is apparent that giving guests choices does not always equal a fabulous time.

At 5:30 we gathered for cocktails, jokes, and to plan for the evening. At least we tried to plan for the evening. Six people assembled on the porch contentedly sipping wine. Four of them gazing at the sun, still high on the horizon and casting magnificent purple shadows across the expanse of mountain ranges. Two of us drinking our wine facing our guests and the gray clapboard house.

"There's a wonderful string quartet in the concert hall at Tanglewood tonight," Joel said with great enthusiasm. "We could take a picnic and eat on the lawn."

"That doesn't do it for me," said Hank, who has been our friend for so long that he never hesitates to say what is on his mind.

"I see in the paper that the new play at the Berkshire Theater Festival has terrific reviews. Let's try to get tickets," I suggested.

"Charles has fallen asleep at the last two plays we've been to," responded Karen. "It's really a waste of time to take him to anything like that."

"Hmmm, let's see," I tried again. "Got it!! I saw that Whitney Houston is singing in a benefit performance at the museum this evening. It's somewhat pricey, but how often do we get to see someone so famous in such an intimate setting? That gets my vote for tonight," I added hopefully.

"I don't know, she gives me a headache with all that screaming," said Ellen.

Figuring, at this point, that a combination of Albert Einstein, Mother Theresa, Robert Redford, and Princess Di would not get a rise out of these people, Joel and I asked if they had any ideas for the evening.

I couldn't believe it – the latest *Star Wars* movie? *Star Wars* it was, ice cream at Bev's Ice Cream Shop afterward, and then home to watch television.

I am wondering if the Almighty is testing my patience. Nights like this are forcing me to love my friends with idiosyncrasies I never realized they had. How come their stuff has never bothered me before? It can only be because I have allowed the burden of their good time to rest on my shoulders. From now on, I will lay the weekend's options on the table well in advance. After we agree, the plans will be set, and by the time the weekend arrives, we will all have a sense of what is coming. Everyone will have a great time without all this last minute fussing about what to do. At least that's the way I see it now.

Who ever thought that having guests would turn out to be a learning experience?

August 24, 1997

This morning I awoke with that Sunday feeling – that sense of hustle and bustle that accompanies the day when our company is ready to head back to their own homes. Joel and I do have terrific people coming to visit, and this group was no exception. I could hear sheets being pulled off beds and then the question "Where are the clean linens?" "Oh, you don't have to bother," I answered, not meaning one word. "Don't be silly," answered Myra, "of course we're changing the linens." Hooray for sensitive guests. Before much time all the beds had been made and towels were stacked neatly in the laundry room hampers. Then the sounds of hangers dropping to the floor and finally the buzz of zippers closing suitcases.

The suitcases were dragged downstairs, Jill's so heavy that poor Dan almost put his back out trying to maneuver the darn thing to the front hall. I didn't know what was bigger, the case with her clothes or the one with her makeup and jewelry. "You only came for two nights," I said, "two nights! You might as well spend the rest of the year." All of us laughed until it hurt except Dan, as he was already hurt. I must remember to give them the first-floor bedroom next time.

Last night, Gloria announced that for breakfast she was going to make Babba's pancakes – a Sunday morning tradition when her children and grandchildren come to visit. By the time I reached the kitchen, two skillets were throwing off the wonderful scent of these exotic treats. Piled high and lightly bathed in dark maple syrup, her efforts signaled a sweet ending to the nicest of weekends.

Breakfast was over and everyone was gathering up their belongings. "Howard, did you see my hairdryer?" asked Gloria. Alan was running out to the porch to pick up the book he was reading last night. "I can't find the car keys." "Will you get the suit bag?" "My camera, where is that damn camera?" And so on, as the anxiety of making sure all belongings were accounted for and thoughts of traffic heading back to the city suddenly intruded on the peace and calm that had pervaded the weekend.

The car keys were found and the camera, as well as a pair of sunglasses that had been missing all weekend. A final picture of the eight of us. The camera was set with a timer that was supposed to go off as we posed. Nothing happened. Alan set it again. Nothing happened. Alan set it again and again and again until we were ready to give up. "One more time," he pleaded, hoping the remote on the camera would work this time, and yes, it finally did.

Hugs and kisses. "Come again soon," Joel said. "Did you sign the guest book?" I asked. "Thanks for a great weekend," they all yelled. And off they went, waving as the cars left the driveway for the last time until next time.

"Love you." "Love you too." The final shouts of friendship diminished as our guests rode out of sight.

Having guests is a lot like childbirth – fortunately you forget the minor discomforts and only remember the wonderful warmth that comes from being close to others. We'll look forward to seeing them next year!

August 31, 1997

I love having old friends visit with us. This weekend has been wonderfully relaxing. Everyone felt comfortable doing what he or she wanted. Sometimes parting is not sweet sorrow but complete bliss. Today we and our guests returned together from activities that appealed to us, rather than feeling the obligation to share every moment of the day.

With shopping, golf, tennis, hiking, or wandering the myriad antique stores behind us, we looked forward to the evening ahead. We gathered on the porch with wine to mellow us out and cheese to satisfy late-day cravings. Soon after, we left each other for a quiet hour or two of reading and napping.

Then, shower after shower, I could hear the water running. This meant less and less hot water for my shower. This also meant more and more towels to be dealt with on Monday morning. Why in the midst of all this good time do I fixate on these stupid thoughts? What part of me is conflicted about the joys and hard work that accompany having guests?

At about seven o'clock, one by one, each couple descended the steps. Refreshed and feeling quite ready for our dinner plan at the Old Inn on the Green, we were soon on our way. One of our favorite restaurants, the Inn is a two-hundred-year-old structure that serves only by candlelight. The rooms are painted with pastoral murals, and each one has a small fireplace original to the building. The flickering candles throw moving shadows on the walls and ceilings. Our host James is convinced that there is a ghost living in the basement and often entertains us with his stories of sightings as well as unexplained noises. Perhaps it is the ghost of Ethan Frome, whose tragic story may have left him wandering the Berkshire Hills in search of peaceful rest. Fact or fantasy, it matters not, as James's encounters add a touch of mystery to this building filled with stories nobody will ever know.

We were seated at our favorite round table in a small room that, except for a couple of tables for two, is essentially our own space. Joel and I took the seats facing the wall, while once again our guests enjoyed the general scenery around us. Our splendid meal did not disappoint us, which is one reason we always enjoy the Inn.

Having guests is surely at its best when sharing a meal at the dinner table, when conversation is stimulating but not overbearing, when the jokes make you guffaw with laughter but do not offend, when the sense of caring is warm and palpable. And having the kind of gracious guests we ask to return over and over again often means never paying for dinner on a Saturday night at your favorite restaurant!

September 21, 1997

This has been a perfect fall weekend. A delicious cool breeze blew through the bedroom window, the air was dry, and the morning sun glistened. "Splendid" was the right word to describe this day. I jumped out of bed so looking forward to all that lay ahead. Perhaps a walk into town to the Red Lion Inn for lunch. The courtyard with its lush flowers and umbrella tables would be an appealing place to relax. Or maybe a picnic and a hike up Monument Mountain, which in reality is more like a steep hill but allows the hiker to bathe in the fantasy of having done something truly noble upon descending from its peak. I ran downstairs ready to tackle breakfast for the gang and get some feedback on my ideas.

Once again, our very thoughtful guests had provided us with bags of special coffees and a groaning board of specialties from Zabar's in New York City. Breakfast on the porch was a feast of smoked salmon, cheeses, wonderful bagels, and fabulous pastries. Just the kind of meal that tells you that a hike up Mount Everest was more in order than what I had in mind.

The meal was in progress, and as Joel and I faced the gray clapboard of our house, I brought up the subject of the day's possible activities. In spite of my best efforts to set weekend activites in advance, there are still those unaccounted times which require some on the spot decisions. "How about a walk into town?" I offered. "We're about 1½ miles from the center of Stockbridge. There are some terrific little shops and the Red Lion awaits us for lunch."

"I am too full to ever think of eating again," came the response from Meredith.

"I can understand that," I said, "but you know that five hours from now you'll be starving. Hey, how abut taking a picnic and hiking up Monument Mountain? The scenery is sensational and we'll all feel that we did something constructive today."

"A hike?" was Harvey's shocked response. "I thought we came to the country to relax. I'll pass on the hike. In fact, I'd rather watch the Giants play the Bills."

"Yeah, I'm in for that activity," chorused the remaining two men.

It was 65 degrees and sunny on this beautiful Berkshire day and half our group opted for watching TV? Well, I figured that the female half would be in for something a little more outdoorsy.

"What do you say, ladies? Shall we leave these turkeys to the television and enjoy our autumn splendor?" I was right about the outdoorsy part but was unprepared for what Audrey and Karen considered outdoors. "We are all for getting out of the house, but we had something different in mind from a hike." I breathlessly awaited news of the expedition we were about to undertake. What I heard was: "Let's go shopping at the discount mall in Lee."

It's taken me a number of years and many guests to get smart. "You're on your own, ladies," I said. "Have a lovely day. See you for cocktails."

September 28, 1997

Yesterday morning Bob and Sonny arrived once again for their semi-annual trip to the Berkshires. With their visit for Tanglewood on Parade behind us, they have returned for our annual autumn wine dinner. We are five couples who have had some of our most memorable moments together with our yearly love affair with the grapes of Bordeaux. With our determination to make this one time of year a sybaritic treat, it is always an embarrassingly luxurious weekend. Friday night we create our own gourmet dinner. Tonight the gustatory extravaganza was at our home. Nothing is too lavish. Terrines of some exotic duck dish and tins (small ones, to be sure) of imported caviar, a conglomerate of courses, one after the other, along with the best wines just perfectly suited to each course. Tonight lived up to the fantasy. By 12:30 in the morning, the Shaws left with their hosts, the Menkers. Believe it or not, the rest of us – in some complete state of lunacy – practically climbed into the freezer to get at Berkshires Best ice cream. Bob and Sonny and our other guests, the Olsteins, giggled their way to their bedrooms. I finished a few details in the kitchen and by one in the morning I had had it. Finally my head hit the pillow.

September 29, 1997

This morning we all awoke looking for the Advil. We decided to try to walk off last night's gustatory debauchery and did what I call the "Joel Stroll" instead of my usual power walk. Just moving was an effort and there was plenty left to the weekend. This afternoon we luxuriated with massages and anticipated the night to come: the be-all and end-all of our bacchanalian weekends – dinner at Blantyre.

I always think that Blantyre shares with Tanglewood the title of "Jewel in the Crown of the Berkshires." To call it a country inn is to belie its grandeur as a world-class establishment in lodging, food, and certainly ambiance. We all tingle each year at the thought of entertaining ourselves at Blantyre for Saturday night dinner. The menu is usually selected by Bob Kohn and Joe Menker and then passed on to the rest of us for agreement or suggestions. The wines are paired by Luk, the hotel's sommelier, who never fails to astonish us with choices that are sublime accompaniments to our meal.

We know to arrive half an hour before our seating. Entering the main salon, we are greeted by the sounds of a harpist plucking gently on his harp, sounds that softly reassure us we are in a place that will offer uncompromised comfort and service. A bar is set up on the opposite side of the harp, and after our coats are taken, we are served flutes of champagne. We enjoy ourselves on deep couches flanking the grand fireplace and partake of bits of delicate hors d'oeuvres. It is quiet. Peacefully quiet.

Soon we are called into dinner, and the real food and wine start their march from kitchen to table. It seems a waste of time for Bob and Joe even to consider other appetizers when we all anticipate the one dish we save for this occasion. Tonight will be no different, I am sure, as we pause to savor the silky smooth texture and light crust of flawlessly seared foie gras sitting, perhaps, on a pool of plum puree or sharing the plate with a side of sautéed apples. Luk will, no doubt, be pouring a deep golden sauterne which, as always, makes us quiver with delight.

At this point, peaceful quiet usually gives way to animated conversation. Upon arrival of the main course, with more wine to drink, animated conversation will no doubt give way to somewhat shrill discussion on topics about which there may be intense differences of opinion. As Luk refills our glasses, shrill discussion may then give way to raucous jokes and screaming laughter, often to Bob's consternation – he once told us in a not too pleasant voice, "You are all disrespecting the wine!" We have never stopped laughing over that line. Eventually loudness, our loudness, drowns everything else out, and inevitably our efficient and gracious servers will discreetly close the door to our small private dining room.

With our dinner plates ready to be removed from the table, we all know the drill. The evening will conclude with coffee, dessert, and conversation in the music room. Finally settled down from all we have consumed, we begin to realize that we are the last patrons to leave, but – no matter the hour – Blantyre's staff would never indicate that we have overstayed our welcome.

As the massive wooden door closes behind us, cool autumn air will jar us back to reality. Tonight's spectacular indulgence will have momentarily removed us all from our own personal issues as well as the greater problems of the outside world. How lucky to be in such a space, even for just an evening.

This is what we have to look forward to tonight. From past experience I know the state of complete exhaustion that will overcome me when we reach home. So, in this quiet hour between my afternoon nap and the time to get dressed, I thought it best to put pen to paper now, otherwise, this story might never find its entry into this journal.

September 30, 1997

This morning I awoke to a bright sun streaming through the bedroom windows. The clock said 8:30 and it felt good to have slept so late. Last night's dinner was way more than a wonderful memory. My throbbing head attested to that. Joel was still snoring happily as I got up and threw on my pretty-in-pink terrycloth robe.

Suddenly the smell of freshly brewed coffee made its way through the kitchen, into the hall, up the stairs, and into my bedroom.

Oh yes, I remembered. Bob is here this weekend, and having guests means fragrant coffee, warm rolls, and pastries from the best bakery in town will surely greet me each morning for the length of his stay.

The house was enveloped in the most luxurious calm and quiet. Joel and Sonny were still curled up in their beds. The Olsteins hadn't been seen. Taking a large mug from the cupboard, I poured myself a searing cup of that delicious brew, grabbed a sticky bun coated with caramelized sugar and studded with pecans, and walked out onto the porch.

Bob also bought the newspapers, and because he and I were alone, guess who got to see the morning sun as it poured its golden light onto the mountains? Sometimes, even with guests, I get to see the view.

Once again, our group reconvened. After Advil and orange juice, we spent our final morning having brunch at the Menkers'. As always, every year seems to be better than the last. Whether this is true or it just feels that way is of no consequence. This feeling is a testament to deeply caring friendships.

In spite of anticipating next year's wine weekend, believe me, dear journal, when I say I am spent. Fortunately, we are all smart enough to keep these mind-bending experiences to a once-a-year phenomenon.

November 24, 1997

It is Tuesday before Thanksgiving. My sister Ronnie and I decided to head up to the country and enjoy two days of girl talk as we prepared for the arrival of the rest of our families and the feast that will follow a few days from now.

For one full week, I have been planning, marketing, cooking, and freezing food for the six days we will spend in the country. Nancy and I made both spinach lasagna and sausage lasagna for Friday's lunch. We baked cookies, pies, and cakes. Because this is the first major holiday in our new home, we are not yet equipped to serve as many as the eighteen people expected for the holiday. So added to the food items, I purchased more glasses, napkins, napkin rings, flatware, serving dishes, and serving pieces. Let's not forget, the card tables and the round tabletops that will add extra seating. That meant we needed more folding chairs as well.

At 6:30 this morning, I woke Joel out of a sound sleep. "Honey, I need help loading the truck," I said. He staggered out of bed, put on his robe and slippers, and sleepily went down to the garage where I heard him roar, "Don't they have stores in the Berkshires?!" His muttering continued through the loading of the coolers of food and all the additional items that piled higher and higher in the truck until all hope of rear window visibility was out of the question. Considering myself well equipped, I added a small bag of personal items, kissed the still muttering Joel goodbye, and headed on out. My meticulous planning ensured that Ronnie and I wouldn't have to face lines in the markets and stores when we reached Stockbridge.

I honked the horn of the Jeep at eight o'clock, a time which Ronnie considers uncivilized at best. I would have liked to start out earlier, but any mention of this idea brought forth unrepeatable words from my sister. So with Ronnie also muttering, we struggled to find room for her suitcase. That done, hallelujah, we were on our way.

Four hours later, as we were unpacking, we began to realize that with all my forethought, we still needed a few things from the market. The list started small, three or four items. This was followed by the inevitable question "Do we have enough of…?", followed by the inevitable answer "We're better off with too much than not enough."

The line in the market was not as long as I thought it would be, and by three in the afternoon, Ronnie and I were settled in for the day. We were like two giddy young girls playing hooky from school. For the moment we had no responsibilities. Laughing and gossiping as only two sisters can, we ate rotisserie chicken and drank white wine standing at the kitchen counter. We watched girly movies that our husbands would sneer at, loving every kissing scene and commenting on the male characters' inability to make a commitment.

Ronnie and I kissed good night. I climbed the stairs limp with exhaustion from the day's work and the evening's laughter. I barely had the energy to write, but knowing me, if I didn't do it now, this page would stay empty forever.

November 25, 1997

I was up at seven this morning, late for me. The house was all peace and quiet. I was alone in the kitchen inhaling the aroma of the day's first cup of coffee, always the cup I enjoy the most. It is my favorite time of day. The phone would not ring for the next hour, and Ronnie would remain tucked in for at least that long. There were no demands to be met and my mind drifted to the passage of the seasons.

Late November is the time of final transition from the memories of summer's heat through the wet coolness of autumn into the bone chilling cold of a New England winter. The wild turkeys that delighted our grandchildren all fall have disappeared, possibly knowing that their days were numbered. However, deer still wander through our property, and we see in them the grace and strength of a prima ballerina.

I became aware that shortly Ronnie and I would be setting tables, cooking two kinds of stuffing, boiling our whole cranberries, and whipping mounds of heavy cream. Candied sweet potatoes, mashed potatoes, and every conceivable fall vegetable would find its way into an endless array of casserole dishes.

We worked tirelessly on the logistics that would keep our families well fed and comfortably active from Thursday through Sunday afternoon. I know that once again, in spite of our efforts, we will wind up in lines at the market and the bakery. It's all a part of the routine, the gearing up, then the greetings and tumult, the laughing, the games, the endless quantities of wonderful food. Then the inevitable agitations and irritations that end in someone yelling as tempers begin to shorten with the passing days. By holiday's end, the sounds of running water will be screaming in my ears. Dishwashers, clothes washers, showers for the adults, the bathtub running for the babies, one load of towels after another. Sometimes I wonder if the well gets as tired of pumping water as I get listening to its constant splash from spigot to basin.

Well, the moment arrived as anticipated. Our parents, my three children, their spouses, and my grandchildren, as well as Ronnie's daughters and sons-in-law were finally here, all smiling and dressed for Thanksgiving dinner. In what felt like an out-of-body experience, I watched the chatter and the interconnectedness of all the generations. In spite of all the work behind us and all the work ahead of us, this moment had indescribable magic. I was indeed thankful for all I saw.

November 29, 1997

Today, Sunday, came not soon enough and yet too soon. Finally, when the last of this group of those I love most waved goodbye and Joel and I were alone, it seemed to be the quietest of all the moments of my life.

In a state of contented exhaustion, I decided to relax in a warm bath. I guess the well was tired after all, for a turn of the faucet released not a single drop of water. The entire house had no running water.

We had all worn out our welcome, and it was not too many hours before Joel and I were back in the Jeep, much emptier now, returning home to New Jersey.

Never mind the well, I thought. Like Scarlett O'Hara, I would think about it tomorrow.

December 31, 1997

While many of our friends have fled to warmer climates to escape the wintry temperatures and the treachery of snow-laden roads, we are nestling deeper and deeper into the coziness of blazing fires, hot soups, and friends who are not afraid of a walk through Tanglewood in frigid conditions.

Streets that teemed with people in the summer and fall of the year are empty of sounds. No longer do we hear giggling children or crying babies. No longer the shouts of grandparents looking for a child who has wandered off, they themselves wondering why they took the kids for a week to begin with. Young couples arm-in-arm have returned to their homes, not to trek back up north until the warmth of a new summer. Trees heavy with foliage that provided needed shade now show only naked branches and the occasional bird looking for seed to nourish it through one more day. It is winter, to be sure, and to some it speaks of loneliness and isolation. This despair is foreign to me and Joel – winter offers us an opportunity to look inward, for quiet contentment, for friends and family to gather without the call of outside activities. We have put thoughts of sports and picnics away with our shorts and sandals.

We are home. This morning I was eagerly waiting to hear the sounds of friends coming to spend New Year's Eve with us. We left the garage door open. They arrived, understanding that the open door was a sign of welcome. "Come in, we are anticipating your company," it told them, even before they have seen us.

Vicki and Ken came along with Nancy and Steve. Lana and Bob followed not long after. Our guests brought carloads of suitcases and shopping bags that held fabulous foods, bottles of wine, chocolates, and cheeses with foreign names, all of which would accompany the dinner I was preparing for our six guests this evening.

Squeals of delight as we greeted each other with hugs and kisses, and an active bustling about as the couples settled into their rooms. This tumultuous enthusiasm created a stark contrast to the absolute stillness that surrounded the Berkshire Hills.

Joel did his part for dinner by adding the extra chairs to the table, after I asked him at least twice. He also made sure there was plenty of ice, after I asked him twice, maybe three times, I can't remember. I don't want to remember because I would just as soon not be annoyed. I find it wise to let some things go. He did make sure there were lots of mixers, limes, and lemons. For this I never have to ask him at all, as he seems obsessed with tonic water and limes.

Two hours later, Brenda and John Martin joined us for cocktails before heading to the Berkshire Bach Society's annual New Year's concert. Joel opened up a bottle of champagne, and we toasted each other as we looked forward to 1998.

I watched everyone lap up the sweet golden squash soup, one spoonful at a time, until I heard the scrape of spoons touching the bottoms of bowls assuring me that time spent in the kitchen had been worth the hard work. Roasted garlic and warm bread were on the table, but not for long. Then I presented the main course of pan-grilled veal chops, new potatoes crisped in the oven with olive oil and fresh rosemary – thanks to Guido's Market – as well as a light and airy broccoli soufflé. I still wonder why I am not Martha Stewart. It had taken some thinking about what I would serve for dessert. Flourless chocolate torte or caramelized almond cake or poached pears on a pool of Kahlua and cream? Mother was right, another champagne problem. The oohs and aahs were my reward.

We finished the evening relaxing in the living room and waiting for the ball to drop in Times Square, which signaled a barrage of kisses and well wishes for the coming year. One final glass of champagne brought our New Year's Eve to a delicious close.

I went to bed looking forward to good things for the coming year, yet we never know what a year will bring. We can only hope for the best.

February 15, 1998

New England is deep into winter these days. Only the hardiest of weekenders continue to venture north in their Ford Broncos, Jeep Cherokees, and Land Rovers. Thickening snow and freezing conditions make road travel hazardous. The days are short and darkness comes so soon that leaving central New Jersey at four o'clock on a Friday afternoon guarantees us a slow and cautious ride up the New York State Thruway.

If we leave during daylight, and particularly after a heavy snow fall, the Taconic State Parkway is our route of choice. Its winding roads take us through miles and miles of quiet country scenery. On sunny days, the snow sparkles like twinkling diamonds, and on gray days the countryside is no less inviting but stark in its beauty. We are then assured of indulging in our fantasies of small towns and warm restaurants waiting just for us at the end of the trip. But safety is a factor in February and the Thruway is the smart option for Joel and me.

We invited Emily and Arnie to join us this weekend. I am always surprised and impressed that friends, especially those who do not ski, are eager to journey to Stockbridge at this time of year. There are, after all, no promises of picnics, boat rides, or music on the lawn at Tanglewood – only the promises of insulated underwear, heavy coats, clearing snow off a cold car, and perhaps a chilling walk from our home down to the Red Lion Inn for breakfast. After blueberry pancakes and coffee, the 1.2 mile walk straight up the hill in freezing weather is often a struggle.

In spite of this, they accept and they accept and they accept, one couple after another, week after week throughout the bleak winter months. And each week I wonder aloud, "What will we do this weekend?" Joel, whose "don't worry, we'll find plenty to do" attitude wreaks havoc with my own compulsive personality, is most often right.

This weekend being like so many, we were on our way northbound. The singular aspect this time of year is the temperature. If it is 20 degrees in New Jersey, it is probably 10 or 15 degrees in the Berkshires. As is our custom we had left the thermostat in our house at a reading of 50 degrees, not exactly a welcoming state for us or our guests.

Not quite so relaxed about freezing his butt off as he is about weekend activities, Joel decided to purchase what has turned out to be a miracle gadget. One of those things you can't even imagine living without. When he dials the house from New Jersey, a computer picks up the phone, Joel enters a few code numbers, a second thermostat is activated and begins to function at a temperature of 70 degrees. I, having no understanding or appreciation of anything more high tech than an answering machine, am constantly expecting to find the house bitter cold upon our arrival. I am happy to say that I have always been wrong, and this Friday evening was no exception. We opened the door to the house, and we instantly felt the warm air being pushed up through the forced air grates in the floor. I still believe it is magic.

Our friends unpacked their bags, and Joel threw some logs on the fireplace in their guest room as well as the one in the living room. Newspaper and a match, and soon the rooms were brilliantly lit with flames of orange and red. Some chardonnay and a few hors d'oeuvres later, we were contented with our friends feeling right at home. After an hour of relaxing, dinner plans became the focus of discussion.

We decided to head down into Great Barrington to Castle Street Café for the best Cornish hen in the area. They also serve the best liver and onions, and the most sublime mashed potatoes. We greeted chef/owner Michael Ballon, who has the distinction of being recognized by the *Wine Spectator* for his excellent selection of wines. We are always tickled by the fact that Michael grew up in our hometown of Scotch Plains, New Jersey. We ordered a smoky cabernet to accompany our dinner. It was a satisfying evening, both the food and our friends.

Saturday morning, I was at my usual spot pouring that most wonderful first cup of coffee. Arnie, who hasn't slept past 5:30 since he was a teenager, came in from the bakery with hot bagels and a local newspaper. The weather channel had informed us that it was 0 degrees with a wind chill of minus 26. We skipped our morning walk.

Arnie's wife Emily and Joel, neither of whom have any understanding of the term "early riser," each made their presence known at about ten o'clock. It is true that opposites attract.

I still had no idea how we were going to spend the next twenty-four hours, but nobody else seemed to care. We were warm and well fed, telling old jokes and talking about new friends.

We finally looked at the *Berkshire Eagle* for the day's activities, and not surprisingly to us, we astonished our guests with a variety of choices. Aston Magna was presenting a program of classical selections at one of the local churches, a poetry reading was taking place in Pittsfield, and the local movie theater had some interesting films.

"Here's something different," said Joel. "Story telling for adults will take place at the Norman Rockwell Museum at six o'clock tonight." Instead of the usual sighs of skepticism, it seemed we were all game for an activity we had not experienced before.

"Look, there is also something that sounds great at the Williamsville Inn," added Emily. "'Jazz singer Vicki True will sing the songs of Sophie Tucker and Billie Holliday. Showtime is at nine o'clock and dinner is offered before the show.' We could go to the story telling and head over to the Inn for dinner and jazz."

Everyone was enthusiastic with this plan. What a terrific night. The first part of our evening was truly something unique. The storyteller was a man about forty years old sporting a long braided ponytail. His checkered flannel shirt and faded jeans made me think of cowboys sitting around a fire during round-up time telling tales to each other in an effort to stifle the boredom that came with empty nights under the stars. He told a story about an old Indian medicine man. He told another about a house that was haunted by the ghost of a murdered young mother. The lights in the lower level of the museum were dim, and the storyteller's voice rose and fell with emotion. He held us spellbound for the better part of an hour. When he completed his final story and the lights came up, it actually took a moment for the audience to return to reality. I also climbed out of my own trance – I'd been completely absorbed in the tales of lives far more intense than my own.

We shivered running to the car. Was it because of the deep freeze that had enveloped us or because some of those eerie stories had sent chills through our veins? The heat in the car finally came up, and we eagerly looked forward to a comforting dinner at the Williamsville Inn and the luscious sounds of Vicki True, whose singing is so beautiful that it could make a songbird blush.

On Sunday we were blessed with milder weather, so we decided on a morning walk. We ventured down to the Red Lion Inn, enjoyed a great brunch, and climbed back up the hill to think about our return trip home.

At two o'clock, Joel set the thermostat down to 50 degrees. Our guests packed their bags, and Joel warmed up the Jeep. We were on our way back to New Jersey.

And that's what we did for the weekend.

March 12, 1998

Clear days of bright sunshine and sharp cold arctic air enter our Berkshire lives sometime in December. Looking towards the holidays, I always play out the coming scenes in my mind. Brunches and dinner parties with family and friends will usher in another new year. Those late December mornings, I am often filled with wellbeing and contentment. A spirit of good cheer inevitably sweeps over me. I wonder in my first-cup-of-coffee morning musings why that time of year feels so good. It must be that I have bought into the dream of all retailers – the need to create holiday fantasy. After all, those brunches mean lots of money spent on fancy foods, and all those beautifully wrapped presents patriotically add to the retail figures the government puts out after the first of the year. Have I really become that cynical? Maybe it is this time of year. March, so flat and gray.

As the winter continues to wear on, the sun seems to slip more and more behind clouds that darken in intensity until weeks have gone by and no light at all seems to filter through. This constant gray chill subdues my spirit and makes me long for spring. We have chosen to remain in New Jersey these last few weeks. The gloom of March is even more pronounced in that silent tundra three hours north.

I feel closeted in my home, cut off from the chance meetings with friends and neighbors we enjoy so casually when nature is in a gentler state. At times it becomes too much of an effort to put on that coat and wrap that scarf tightly around my neck just to go to a movie. More often than not, I convince Joel to rent some videos and hunker down on our couch.

There came a moment, this morning, in all this grimness, when I needed to join the flock of humanity once more. I suddenly wished to head over to the corner café that serves as our informal meeting place in my New Jersey neighborhood. It is always certain that someone will be there for a cup of coffee and easygoing conversation. This is the place where news travels. Engagements are revealed and new grandparents have baby pictures to show. We also discover who has recently divorced and who has married for the third time. Information emerges about so-and-so who sold his business for millions and what's-their-names who lost everything, declaring bankruptcy and moving to Florida. We find out which souls have been dealing with terrible illness and delight in hearing which of them is responding so well to a new treatment. But most poignant of all, I learn of those who have suffered and have passed on, leaving their suffering behind. This time it was an acquaintance in her mid-fifties, succumbing to the cancer that turned a once vibrant human being into a person broken with pain and despair. She left this world at a time of her own choosing, by sitting in the car with the garage doors closed and the motor running.

The casual air of camaraderie came to a harsh end. Not what I had hoped for when I bundled up for that cup of coffee with friends. We had gathered to find some light in the bleak skies of early March. It was actually bleaker than we had imagined.

The wind seemed especially fierce today. The groundhog was right last month – there is still plenty of winter left.

April 9, 1998

Every fall, I look forward to the confinement to home and hearth that comes with winter's harshness. Heavy coats and insulated mittens fail to fend off the bitter cold, and we are soon driven back into our homes. The kitchen, that long abandoned outpost we left for summer barbeques and picnics, now beckons me to cook huge pots of soups and stews to be eaten fireside with a red wine.

By the middle of last month, much of winter's delight had worn thin and thoughts of sandals and sleeveless blouses began to have their appeal. April is coming. The crocus and daffodil will peer up at any time now to comfort us with the knowledge that nature is indeed cyclical. Yes, easier days are coming. Or are they?

April is a soft word. It has soft sounds. It carries with it the sweetness of gentle rains and light breezes, longer days, clearer skies, the sun in all its glory. I am anticipating the warmth to come.

This is the month that often seems to me to be life's little joke. I know what July and August are about. The heat of summer months is a certainty. The fall months are almost always refreshingly inviting in their crispness and variegated color. We usually have a clear picture of what winter has in store for us – cold, cold, and more cold, packaged with what starts out as enchanting snow and ends up as slippery ugly slush.

And here it is, April, like a failed romance, overflowing with promises never kept. The crocus dies under a sudden frost. The rains are heavy and the dampness keeps an unrelenting rawness in the air. The soggy ground underfoot finds me in waterproof boots and shoes long after my thoughts have turned to those sandals. And to add misery to more misery, it is not uncommon for March winds to pound at us in April as well. Last week's odd April snowstorm just put me in the bleakest of moods. Those longing-for-springtime blues hit me hard. I reluctantly kept woolen sweaters and heavy coats close at hand when I really wanted to put them in the basement closet, or even more emphatically I was ready to put them in the Goodwill box. My hunger for a gentler climate seemed to increase as the disappointing days of April inched on.

And then this morning I opened my eyes and had to blink for the rays of a strong sun unexpectedly made me squint. I turned on the weather channel, and there it was: 55 degrees and sunny with an expected high of 62. It was warm and dry and ever so inviting to my soul to know that nature is ready to offer the balm that belongs to the first days of spring.

The new cycle is ready to begin again.

May 14, 1998

This morning I decided that it was time to revisit a place I hadn't been to in a number of years. I had mentioned to Joel at one time that it would be nice to see Benmarl Winery again and say hello to Mark Miller, the proprietor. The winery – in Marlboro, New York, in the heart of the Hudson Valley – is not very far out of our way. Joel had not been interested in taking this detour, but today I was the driver and he had fallen asleep in the passenger seat, so I just veered off Route 84 onto Route 9W (not to be confused with routes 9, 9E, 9H, or 9D) and drove north for a few miles until I reached the familiar turn that took us up the hill to Benmarl.

The vineyard is set high above acres of apple orchards, for which New York State is famous. This morning the apple trees provided my eyes with the flurry of white blossoms that precede the fruit, which will be picked around October. The branches swayed under a warm spring breeze, and the last of the white petals were gently blown everywhere, as if a light snow had descended upon the northeast in May. I drove the winding dirt road past the grape vines languidly hanging from their wired posts. Memories of years ago were instantly recalled.

Nancy was sixteen, and I was working as a guidance counselor/social worker at Millburn High School. I wanted to find an activity for us to share alone, and for no particular reason I decided we should take a wine course together. So each Tuesday evening, Nancy and I took the number 113 bus into New York City for a course on Burgundy wines. The lessons gave detailed history of that part of the French wine country known for its great pinot noirs and chardonnays. We learned about soil and climate. We learned about grape varietals and exactly how wine is made from those grape varietals. We also tasted wines. Lots of wines during the entire evening. This was the reason Nancy and I took the bus into the City and had Joel pick us up each week – I was a little too buzzed to get us home on our own. I guess, in retrospect, it was an odd thing for a mother to do with her sixteen-year-old daughter – and on a weeknight, especially out of the ordinary.

Week after week, Nancy and I became more invested in all the nuances that take a small red fruit and nurture that fruit into some of the world's most spectacular and expensive wines. By the time the first class was over, Nancy had decided that she wanted to spend some time working in a vineyard. This was the perfect experience for her to complete a six-week off-campus program required for her senior year of high school. The young couple who taught the wine classes had some affiliation with a winery in New York State. They made a recommendation to Mark and Dene Miller, and soon Nancy had an invitation to work at Benmarl for four of the six weeks of her program. She was to spend the final two weeks working at a wholesale distributor of fine wines and liquors.

Benmarl is, to this day, the oldest functioning farm winery in the country. The Millers purchased it after their return from a number of years in Burgundy. It was Mark's dream to grow and blend wines in the Hudson Valley in the style of Burgundy's best. The finest varietals come from the vinifera family of vines, which are not generally suited to New York's cold winters, so Mark planted hybrid vines that would tolerate the climate. He was not only a dedicated vintner, but a well respected illustrator who, in his early life, had his work on the covers of leading magazines.

Nancy was graciously received by the Millers and worked so hard in the vineyards that they named the 1984 bottling Nancy's Vine. A relationship developed, and for a number of years after, she and I volunteered our time helping out with the spring and fall tastings. We would arrive early on Saturday morning, set up our stations, and wait for the public to arrive and sample Mark and Dene's latest efforts. A counter was loaded with enticing baked goods, coffee, and of course plenty of wine, mostly white and chilled, to be enjoyed with the picnic lunches carried in by the guests.

The days usually went by swiftly as we enthusiastically presented the wines, encouraging people to place their orders before leaving. By the time five o'clock came and the last of the visitors had left, we were exhausted. It was about then that Dene would call us into the house for dinner around the big farm table. Dinner was the kind of affair that would have satisfied hungry cowhands who had spent their day herding cattle from sunup till sundown. Huge slabs of blood-rare roast beef, steam table–sized platters of Yorkshire pudding, enormous bowls of vegetables glazed with melted butter oozing over each carrot, string bean, and broccoli floret. When I remember those nights, I can still hear the steady pour of the wine from bottle to glass, a never ending stream of deep purple liquid that tasted not only of the fruit of the grape, but of apples and spices, and smelled of the earth.

Nancy went off to college and our visits to the winery lessened until there came a time when we just couldn't manage to get there anymore. Life took us in another direction. Then Dene became ill with pancreatic cancer, and three months after, she saw her last fall tasting.

Each week for the last two months we have passed through Newburgh on our way to the Berkshire house. My longing to go once more to Benmarl had intensified every time I read the sign for Route 9W North. I hoped Mark would be around. I had heard he had remarried, and I wondered if his wife had settled into the vineyard and was now preparing the feasts that satisfied workers after the tastings. We pulled into the familiar parking area. Joel suddenly woke up. "What are we doing here?" he demanded, agitated. "I've been needing to come back here," I told him, "and since I was driving, I made the choice to stop here and grab a few memories. Come on, let's go find Mark."

Things were quiet although the winery welcomes visitors every day. There Mark was, wearing faded jeans, a plaid shirt, and slouched hat. He ran over to us and threw his arms around me with a hug that made me feel as if I had never been away. "So great to see you," he said, asking, "What brings you here?" "I just needed to come back and say hello. It has been so long. How are you?" I asked. "Just fine. Looking forward to picking the grapes in few weeks, hoping the sun will keep shining and that we don't get any major hurricanes that will water down the grapes. Every year is a guessing game. Some years we win and some years let us down. Come in and meet my wife. I think you'll like her."

We followed Mark into the house and an attractive blonde woman with short hair and a broad smile greeted us. Mark introduced us to Grace. One look and it was easily apparent that they were happy together. Their eyes met and they looked so delighted to see each other, as if they had been apart for much longer than the couple of hours Mark had been in the vineyard this morning.

Courtesy of Benmarl Winery, Marlboro, NY

They both took pleasure in showing us around new tasting rooms and wine cellars, and taking us on a walk through the vines. The short visit was over but not before we were given a gift of the best of the most recent Baco Noir bottling. Of course we made promises that we would not be "strangers" and would return soon. Mark asked us to send Nancy his love. Who knows? Maybe I can talk Nancy into coming back with me in October for the fall tasting.

Joel and I left reminiscing about "Nancy's Vine," which we served to toast our daughter and her new husband at their wedding in 1987. Joel was in better humor but still insisted on driving the rest of the way home to avoid any other unwelcome stops.

June 10, 1998

Our guests had the greatest weekend. At least all the screaming and guffawing made me think so. They had been well treated. No alarms woke them up. And when they did rouse themselves, most of the restless sleepers declared that they had never slept better. This morning, an ordinary Sunday morning, aromas of bacon sautéing in the skillet and blueberry peach cake just out of the oven enveloped the house in the comforting smells of home cooking. The farm table was set on the porch. Our friends emerged from their cocoons to find their places at the table. So relaxed, so calm, so unsuspecting that they were about to be assaulted by The Dreaded Guest Book.

"Hi, everyone," I said in my softest voice. "Breakfast is just about ready, but would you do one thing for me as soon as we finish eating?" "Sure," they said, probably thinking I needed someone to help in the kitchen or something else along those lines. I had nothing so benign in mind. "Would you put a few words about the weekend in our guest book?" "Of course, we'd love to," answered Jeannie, and the other three chimed in that it would be fun.

Well, breakfast was over, and we saw no one for the next two hours. Deciding what to write in the guest book had transformed our guests' relaxed and calm demeanor into one of sheer terror. Our friends had suddenly become aware of the fact that their written comments would be forever stamped in that book. Their words in indelible pen would be read and admired or critiqued by those who came after them. Their ability to express themselves with emotion or humor, and to do it with great creativity had, in one instant, instilled unexpected turmoil.

Morning came to a close and Sue Ellen was still locked in her room. We sent her husband, Todd, to see if she was OK. "Just putting the finishing touches on the guest book entry," he remarked upon returning to the living room. Soon a haggard Sue Ellen appeared, book in hand. We read the entry and delighted in all she wrote. The look of relief on her face made me wonder what cruel part of my personality inflicts my guest book on people week after week. I love reading the entries many times during the year, but does this entitle me to require that my guests indulge me at such emotional peril to themselves? I think it must remind them of the pressure we used to feel on the last day of elementary school when we wrote notes and rhymes in autograph books. Later, in high school, we would sign each other's yearbooks, always trying to write the cleverest, brightest, or funniest entry. We seem to have survived that trauma. I am sure the guest book will not leave any lasting psychological marks either.

The last of the bags and golf clubs were in the cars, and, as our guests left, I wondered if any of them would ever come back.

July 9, 1998

Every guest feels it is his or her responsibility to bring a gift to our home. Sometimes I wish that it were simply bathroom tissue, napkins, or paper towels. As much as I insist that a gift is not necessary, we have a cupboard full of lovely things given with great affection. Soon we will be able to open our own shop, overflowing as we are with ceramic bowls, beaded napkin rings, placemats, trays, cheese boards, spreaders, corkscrews, and wine coasters. I would be embarrassed for anyone to know that I have actually started to give some of these things to others. I make sure that I keep the giver's card in the box, so I don't return the gift to the person who was kind enough to take the time to get me something she thought I might enjoy. Actually, for all I know, maybe those gifts have been recycled as well. No matter how I insist, our gracious guests keep bringing items that I receive with false glee and which get put away after they leave only to be retrieved when they visit again.

During the week Roz Wolcott called to firm up plans for this weekend. "Did I catch you at a bad time?" she asked. "No, just browning some chicken for dinner," I answered. "By the way, don't bring me anything, please. All we want is your company."

While we were chatting about what to wear and what time they would arrive, I turned up the flame under the pot just enough to get the poultry to brown a bit more. Walking away to get my calendar with the weekend's activities, I left the large pot hissing with the promise of a crusty caramelized skin on my chicken.

A little gossip, some more discussion, and before I knew it I had forgotten about the pot still on the burner. Suddenly that unexpected smoky odor that all cooks fear found its way to my nose. "The pot is burning," I screamed into the phone as I ran to the kitchen. In my rush I simply slammed the phone on Roz and dealt with the burnt meat and the pot, which had been destroyed. Hoping the fog of smoke and the unwanted smell of burnt food would vanish in my absence, I left the house with fans on and windows open. My destination was the Price Chopper market to buy one of their ready-cooked roasters.

Yup, I do have the best friends. The Wolcotts and the Rodmans arrived yesterday and with them was the best gift of all – a fabulous Le Creuset Dutch oven. Preparing stews and soups will be all the more special because of the friends whose thoughtfulness replaced the charred remains of my old pot.

It has become apparent that having guests is learning the art of diplomacy in order that each person invited into our home feels that the chosen gift is the item we wanted most in the world. Sometimes it is!

August 24, 1998

We spent this last week at our home in New Jersey. It was wonderful to be with friends we haven't seen all summer, but at week's end we were glad to return to the Berkshires. Time and again the New Jersey gang asked the same question: "What do you do up there all summer?" They seem to think we live in some vacuum of nothingness. "Come and check it out," I say to those who are forever reluctant to give something new a chance. "I like my own bed," or "I have my games on the weekends," or "I can't stand the thought of fighting traffic." These are the responses that annoyed me the whole week. All the questions have made me aware of how many goings-on we have up here. I've decided to write a letter to my skeptical friends south of the border to refute their provincial ideas about what life is like here in this fabulous country environment. I will overwhelm them with details about the diversity of activities and fine entertainment. By the time they read my letter, they will be embarrassed to ever again ask the question "What do you do up there?"

Dear Friends,

In answer to your questions regarding how we keep busy in the Berkshires, I thought it might be helpful if you had some understanding of what entices me and Joel to drive three hours north each weekend. So, for your information:

Excellent theater is available at a number of venues, most notably the Berkshire Theatre Festival, Shakespeare and Co., and Barrington Stage Co. The BTF has been one of the finest summer stock theaters in the United States for more than fifty years. An amazing array of stars from both stage and screen have found it a privilege to grace its stage, Joanne Woodward and Richard Chamberlain being two that come to mind. The BTF has shown its influence by sending a number of shows from the Berkshires to Broadway and Off Broadway.

Shakespeare and Co. performs an extraordinary service to the public with its successful effort to keep the works of William Shakespeare alive and well in surroundings that invite all to keep returning. Currently this repertory company performs its plays at the Mount, the magnificent estate which was built by Edith Wharton and her then-husband Teddy. The Mount itself is undergoing constant renovation, and its grounds and mansion as well as the stables complete an enchanting backdrop for a variety of productions which suit many tastes. In addition to her dedication to the Bard, artistic director Tina Packer brings together a repertory of short works by Edith Wharton and other playwrights of note. Every year on July 4th, the company treats the community to a reading of the Declaration of Independence. It took Joel and me several years to get to this reading, which we found so moving and inspiring that we will make this an annual event and bring our guests with us.

Dance, of course, is most magnificently experienced at the world acclaimed Jacob's Pillow. This theater, tucked into the wooded setting of Becket, Massachusetts, brings performances by the country's premier dance troupes to our area of the country.

Music, however, created the magic in the Berkshires when a group of wealthy people decided to establish a permanent summer home for the Boston Symphony Orchestra. In the 1940s, the music Shed at Tanglewood was built for Serge Koussevitzky, then the beloved conductor of the BSO. Tanglewood continues to be the most revered of all the summer music festivals. Over the years, its mission has evolved to include programs that teach and encourage fine young professional musicians. The mission even extends itself to working with talented high school students through the Boston University Tanglewood Institute. Music does not stop with instruments, and the training of those with vocal talents has a place in the choral program. For eight weeks each summer, the hills are alive with the sound of music.

No small contribution to the music in the Berkshires are a number of venues for chamber concerts of exceptional quality. They take place at Searles Castle in Great Barrington, at Seven Hills Inn in Lenox, at Tannery Pond and many other places too numerous to mention. Six times a year in late fall, the Berkshires is treated to a series of classical concerts called "Close Encounters with Music," founded by Yehuda Hanani. Mr. Hanani, an accomplished cellist, brings together world class musicians performing chamber music in Great Barrington's St. James Church. Hanani begins each event with an informative and often humorous monologue abut the program. The performances are followed by a reception to which the entire audience is graciously invited.

There are, at various times, extraordinary opera productions and any number of jazz concerts, not the least of which is the Labor Day weekend Jazz Festival at Tanglewood.

Museums abound, with the Norman Rockwell Museum being the most well known. Designed by Robert A.M. Stern, this neo-classical structure houses Rockwell's collection of paintings, which captures the essence of America and the American dream. Museum curator Laurie Moffat does a superb job of combining the permanent Rockwell paintings with fascinating exhibits by other artists.

Across from the Rockwell, a country road leads to Chesterwood, the home of noted sculptor Daniel Chester French. French created the Lincoln Memorial which stands in Washington, D.C. His home and studio are open to the public. Another activity not to be missed, if time permits.

The Berkshire Museum, in Pittsfield, has the most intriguing rotating exhibits. Our grandchildren were enchanted by the hands-on exhibit called "Sprockets, Springs, and Pulleys." An aquarium housed on the ground floor is another draw for children and adults alike.

Pittsfield also boasts "Arrowhead," the home occupied by Herman Melville and his family. It was here that he wrote his epic *Moby Dick*. His friend Nathaniel Hawthorne had encouraged Melville to reside in Berkshire County.

Since we live in Southern Berkshire County, our concentration of activities lies in this area. But, if you are still needing more interesting places to visit, just keep riding Route 7 North to Northern Berkshire County. You will pass Hancock Shaker Village and eventually get to Williamstown and Williams College, which houses the famous Clark Museum. Summer stock theater at the college is well worth the trip north. Recently a group of old warehouses has been restored to create a new art and music center. Called Mass MoCA, it is drawing crowds to the town of North Adams. The revitalization of North Adams has been helped along with excellent restaurants and the Porches Inn, which seems to be the place to stay in that area.

It wouldn't do to leave out two attractions that are favorites with our women guests: the discount mall in Lee and the great antiquing along Route 7 from Great Barrington south into Sheffield.

Still more venues are in the beginning stages of revitalization. The old Mahaiwe Theatre in Great Barrington and the former Colonial Theatre in Pittsfield are undergoing preliminary renovations that will restore them to the grandeur of half a century ago.

And for those of you have trouble with all things cerebral, you can content yourselves with golf, boating, fishing, tennis, riding the rapids, and even horseback riding.

And last but surely not least, the Berkshires is home to a wide variety of charities. People up here are socially conscious and give freely of their time and energy to help others. We have organizations such as Construct, which supports efforts to aid the homeless, and Volunteers in Medicine, seeing to the health and wellbeing of those who could not otherwise receive the right medical attention. There are so many places we can be of use, that boredom is not an option.

Well, dear friends, I hope this puts to rest your concerns about our well-being away from the great metropolitan area. The only problem we have is choosing where to put ourselves every day and night. You all know what my mother, Lillian, would say "It's only a champagne problem, dear.

Love,
Gayle

Maybe when they read this our friends will take the next step and actually come and see for themselves. Maybe I don't want them to come. Maybe the pressure of having to impress those who would rather remain unimpressed is more than I need. I think I should content myself with the friends who delight in sharing our Berkshire experience. Yes, what do I need the others for? Let them stay home.

September 21, 1998

When we left the Berkshires after Labor Day, two weeks ago, the town was completely intact. When we drove through town this morning, the Stockbridge Market and Café was dark and vacant. The historic market space, above which Normal Rockwell had his first studio, and which – last summer – Nina and Moshe took over with such enthusiastic and hopeful energy, was closed. Permanently. I was overcome by sadness for the death of dreams that were so alive not but a year ago.

I was afraid this would happen. Stockbridge is a wonderful tourist town, but only 2,000 people claim permanent residency. Weekenders do swell our numbers, but it is still, by all standards, a small community. In the summertime, Stockbridge overflows with visitors, many lured by the Red Lion Inn. Besides the Inn, we have the small but well stocked Shanahan's Elm Street Market and also Nejaimes, a great wine and cheese shop. It seems doubtful that Stockbridge can support another market. In spite of the odds, over the years a number of hopefuls have valiantly tried to make a success of it.

I remember pulling into town one Friday afternoon late last spring and being cheered by the sight of activity through the previously empty store window. On closer inspection Joel and I detected the bustle of hammering and sawing, and stopped to investigate.

"Yes, the market will open shortly," said an earnest young woman with a mane of curly dark hair. Nina and her husband, Moshe, were constructing for themselves and their family a new life in a new place. Moshe, Israeli by birth, and Nina, an American, had lived in Israel for many years. As time passed, Nina felt a need to return to the United States. With two young teenagers left in the care of family, Nina and Moshe searched for a quiet and safe environment and ultimately came to Southern Berkshire County for their new beginning. A broad smile brightened Nina's face as she spoke of their plans that spring afternoon.

I wished her well and went on my way, feeling a lump in my throat. A great deal in the lives of these two people was dependent on the success of what would be called the Stockbridge Market and Café.

I spent the summer of '97 watching as Nina and Moshe launched their new venture. They painted and enlarged the café area. They bought dishes with charming country scenes and spread checkered clothes over the tables. They stocked the grocery shelves and added a fresh baked-goods counter filled with the morning's muffins and breads from the area's best bakeries. The meat and deli counters were sparse, but it was hard to make a commitment to expensive perishables until Nina and Moshe were sure they had a clientele for such items. I watched them as if they were related to me. I hoped for their success and bought from them every chance I could, even if it meant paying more for bathroom tissue and toothpaste than if I had shopped at the large Price Chopper in Great Barrington.

One Monday morning, I walked into town and headed straight to the café for breakfast. Monday mornings the café area was always busy: Weekend tourists were filling their bellies, as well as their gas tanks, in readiness for the journey back to "civilization." The sight almost broke my heart. People calling out for a check so they might be on their way, others holding up generous coffee mugs for refills, still others waiting on line to be seated, while dirty tables lay in wait for someone to tend to them. One waitress apologizing for serving the wrong order and then apologizing for an order that was never served. I looked at the cooking station and there seemed to be utter confusion. I saw despair in Nina's eyes as she said that two of her helpers had called in sick. She went on to explain that the old grill, which had come with the building, had given out. It occurred to me she could be the next thing to give out.

I was plenty used to kitchen work, and since I was on my own with no place to go, I asked if she would like my help. It would have been one of those moments to put pride on the back burner, so to speak, for Nina and Moshe surely needed an extra pair of hands. But my offer was politely declined with the assurance that other workers were on their way to fill in.

Wondering anxiously, I walked back up the hill.

A year went by. Nina and Moshe continued to make improvements to the market. They added spiffy pine shelving and a variety of gourmet items, fine coffees and jams, as well as fresh-squeezed juice from Guido's in Pittsfield. As that summer moved along, they offered rotisserie chickens and Tanglewood picnic baskets.

They really really tried, but their forced smiles and exhausted expressions told a tale of too much effort for too little return on their investments, both time and money.

"How are things going?" I would ask occasionally. "Not too bad now, but I don't know what will happen after the summer season," Nina answered one day. And as August began to dwindle, the stock on the shelves also began to dwindle. One day, the meat and deli counter were covered with butchers paper that signaled the end of rotisserie chickens and Tanglewood picnic baskets.

As hot sticky August moved along and the days imperceptibly became shorter, Nina and Moshe's shelves continued to become more and more sparse. So it went, item by item that was not replaced: grocery, dairy, frozen foods, cereal boxes, bug repellent.

When we left Stockbridge on Labor Day – at the end of the summer and before the fall foliage season – I knew we'd be returning to a different town. In mid-September the Berkshires takes on a temporary air of quiet, with the Boston Symphony and the Berkshire Theatre Festival, our two major cultural barometers of the summer, having completed their seasons. But I had not known that it would be the last time I would see Nina and Moshe. They're gone. It is two weeks later and indeed the season is over – for some more than others.

November 20, 1998

We rode into the Berkshires at around seven this evening. It is Friday, which means Elm Court night. The crowd was there, getting ready to break up into groups of six and eight for dinner. We tacked on to a group of six. So much fun. I am always amazed at the developments in life that happen by chance.

By now Joel and I have eaten our way through a veritable alphabet of Berkshire restaurants, from Aegean Breeze (a welcome wind blew this wonderful restaurant into town) all the way to Zinc (a great little bistro in Lenox). On our way from A to Z, we latched on to one of the best restaurants in the area. The Elm Court Inn, owned by Glee and Urs Bieri, has become one of our favorite places. Urs, former head chef at the United Nations, turns a meal into a fabulous gustatory experience. Always wanting our guests to have a great time means dinner at the Elm Court during their stay with us. Urs's food is never less than outstanding, so naturally we started to eat there with more and more frequency. There are some winter's weekends when we eat in the bar two nights in a row.

The bartender, one Cathy Gordon, is a woman we have known for many years. Personable and attractive, Cathy is a friend to all and a special friend to the bar crowd at the Elm Court. One November night, in casual conversation with Cathy, Joel mentioned that we had some fine Bordeaux wines he would like to sell. In less time than it takes to say Chateau Lafite, Cathy introduced Joel to Woody.

Woody and Marjorie Sumner are among the movers and shakers of the Elm Court Crowd. Woody is a man with great passions – wine, king among them. Joel and Woody hit it off – I might say they fell in love with one another. While no wine was sold, a friendship was sealed. Our Cathy, seeing the affinity these two guys had for one another, invited us to her home for a dinner party. Included in this party were Anne and Ernie Schnessel, better known as the Baron and Baroness von Schnessel, as well as George Minkoff, brilliant mind extraordinaire, and most certainly the Sumners.

What a time we had. Over-indulgence was the order of the evening. Cathy is an inventive cook but has trouble with portion size. Ten pounds of spinach, even wilted, is a little much for eight people. The gargantuan amount of the green stuff notwithstanding, the food was wonderful. Woody, whose zest for life drives him to excess, came in with three bottles of wine and two bottles of champagne, also meant to be consumed by the same eight people who were supposed to eat ten pounds of spinach.

The self-appointed Baron Ernie and Baroness Anne have become fast friends. Committed travelers, they intrigued us with stories about adventures in the Galapagos. I am a timid sort, always happiest when I am in familiar territory, often worried that the cab driver in a foreign land is actually kidnapping us and we will wake up with a light swinging above our heads in some abandoned port. So I was really impressed with Anne, who went on such a physically demanding trip – with a broken leg, no less. Then they told us about their trip to Iran. This really unnerved me. Jews in Iran? Once again I was in awe of Anne, who spent the entire week in a chador, the complete covering required of women in Iran. Often I wish I had a bit of courage, just enough to ride that elephant deep into the forest of Thailand to see the Hmong tribe, which is what Joel did while I read a book in the safety of the campground. Unfortunately, I really do understand the cowardly lion.

George has a wit and a fund of knowledge unmatched by other humans. I have found, sometimes to my annoyance, that George knows everything about everything. If I can't think of who wrote *The Greek Way*, George will be ready to inform me that it was Edith Hamilton.

Marjorie, Woody's wife, a successful real estate broker, handles people with a graceful charm that serves as a much needed balance to her husband's zany personality. She remains calm when he comes home with another antique car or leaves for a golf game wearing knickers, knee socks, and a cap. His decision to become a producer of live entertainment was Marjorie's latest surprise. Much to her delight, his company Destiny Productions is filling local performing arts centers with great jazz and blues acts. Life with Woody is an adventure, and Marjorie seems to enjoy the roller coaster.

While I am thinking about that evening, Cathy, the gatherer of people, has her own interesting story. I think Cathy can accomplish anything she sets out to do. I, who have struggled with golf for so many years, could not believe that Cathy just dropped the sport one day. She was a 14-handicap golfer and, unlike me, must have made her golfing father a happy guy. But it seems one day she decided she would rather paint. Just like that. I can't even imagine. Now her work sells regularly in one of the area galleries. Joel and I bought a piece right off her wall. A stark scene of a large tree, barren of leaves, set in the depth of a snowy winter.

Joel added to the evening as well. He tells a great joke and begins laughing even before he has finished. His guffaws get everyone else hysterical and soon the punch line is secondary to the howls coming from Joel. His great laugh is just as winning when someone else tells a story. This side of him always makes me see an attractive willingness to engage and be engaged by others.

That first night at Cathy's house was the beginning of how we came to enjoy the company of this group of Berkshire friends. We have easily fallen into the Friday-night-at-the-Elm-Court habit. Tonight was no exception, and when we pulled into the parking lot we saw the familiar cars of the gang waiting inside.

As time has gone by, we have met so many wonderful new friends who are part of the Elm Court crowd. Unique in personality and occupation, all have come to the Berkshires from different areas. Each person has a particular talent that creates an atmosphere of great diversity.

We have learned the hard way that politics is not a subject to be discussed, but it seems to come up even though everyone understands that neither the staunch liberals nor the arch-conservatives will win any converts. Some nights have become heated past the point of differences of opinion. Joel, Woody, and George hold up the Republican end, and the Schnessels are not alone in their opposition to conservative philosophy. Bernie and Ethel Norton have strong ties to the Democrats, and

Bernie and Joel like to go at it. Neither Ethel nor I like to listen to this nonsense hour after hour, but we seem powerless to stop it.

I have spent a lifetime trying to get Joel to stop talking politics. His determination to sway people to his point of view is an addiction that seems to intrude on every dinner conversation we've ever had. Most of the time, it upsets me more than anyone else. I am always waiting for the argument to intensify, and from nervous anticipation I start eating bread. I keep telling Joel that if this keeps up, we will have no friends and I will weigh 300 pounds. Does he listen? No. So what's new?

This evening we sat with the Nortons and the Silbersteins. Elaine Silberstein is an interior designer. I have seen two houses that she has done, and I like her work very much. She seems to have an intuitive sense of what a space needs to complete the picture in her client's mind. Len, Elaine's husband, has an interest in spirituality and often initiates discussion of topics with which I am not all that familiar. He has taught me some things about the Hebrew mysticism of Kabala, the same Kabala that seems to have intrigued stars such as Madonna. These are the conversations that educate and entertain. How different than so many nights spent talking about restaurants and clothes and plans for someone's next trip.

Of course with Joel at the table and two couples who are liberal Democrats, the talk eventually turned to politics. Once again Ethel and I pleaded with the guys to talk about anything else. I would even have welcomed restaurants and clothes. It is sometimes impossible to change the subject when these guys get going and the entire evening becomes consumed by this one topic.

These Friday nights have become a special tradition, but boy am I stuffed from all that bread.

January 1, 1999

Last night was New Year's Eve. Almost all of our New Years have been spent with my friend Vicki. Many years ago we spent the night with Vicki and her first husband Barry Snyder. We were three couples, including Bob and Harlene Hoffman. Each year for many years we would spend two nights in New York City. Seeing shows, going to the Philharmonic, wandering around the city shopping and eating was a great way to leave one year behind and enter the year ahead. We had some hilarious times, like the evening we thought we hired an elegant limousine. We exited the theater, ran into some people we knew, and felt quite important that our limousine was waiting for us. Suddenly we heard a roar. "Looking for the Snyder party," a voice barreled across the street. Everyone in front of the theater stopped and looked. If we had thought about it, we probably would have pretended that it was a different Snyder, not our group. We were so distressed and self-conscious that our instant reaction was to run to the car to try to minimize the damage by shutting this guy up. To add to our humiliation, the "chauffer" was an enormous Texan who wore a huge cowboy hat and had his girlfriend in the front seat. The "limo" was banged up in three places and our Texas Ranger continued to bellow at us like we were his wayward children. Some things are worth the momentary agony, I guess, as this night has given us years of laughter.

When Vicki and Barry decided to go their own separate ways, Vicki got custody of Joel and me, and that is how we have come to spend the past many New Years with her and her husband Ken Wolff. This year they went to visit Ken's daughter in Colorado, so our calendar was free until Marilyn Kraft decided to have a late cocktail and dessert party.

Our group of six couples decided to attend the annual Berkshire Bach Society concert held at the Consolati Auditorium. This being the week after the winter solstice, it was pitch black at 5:30 when the Dorns picked us up and we headed the short distance south to Sheffield. We were wrapped securely against December's chill and walking gingerly overly the slippery layer of newly fallen snow. The concert, as always, was sold out as the group does an exceptional job of playing the six Brandenburg concertos. They are wonderful pieces, but frankly I think Bach probably could have stopped at four. I always have trouble keeping my eyes open for the last two pieces, and it's a little embarrassing to have to shake Joel so that he stops snoring.

Now that I think about it, I find most things are too long. Even a great movie is usually fifteen minutes too long. I've barely seen a Broadway play that couldn't have been cut by a good twenty minutes without compromising the show – especially musicals when they start singing a song for the second time. I think that's what they call the reprise. Why do we need to listen to the same tune again? Doesn't the director think we got it the first time? Even the game of golf could be shortened by three holes and would anybody care? Of course not – most people are miserable by the eighteenth hole anyway. Why not diminish the agony of waiting for lunch? So if I could e-mail Bach, I would tell to go easy on so many concertos. I would tell Beethoven not to knock himself out with such a plethora of piano sonatas. I believe there are eighteen of them, and after two or three I think they all sound alike. Anyway, as usual nobody asked for my opinion.

In spite of my complaining about the length of the concertos, I really looked forward to the evening because we don't get much of a chance to spend time with this group of Berkshire friends introduced to us a few years ago by Charlotte and Sheldon Gross. We always seem to be on opposite schedules, but last night should have worked out better than it did.

A call at six o'clock, just before we were set to leave, informed me of a tragedy that had befallen an old friend of ours. Her son was found dead yesterday afternoon. They didn't know what happened. I was in shock. I hadn't seen this young man in a while, but I had known him since he was a small boy. The horn sounded, and we went on with the evening as planned, though both Joel and I were shaken. We decided not to share such tragic information with this group, none of whom really know our grief-stricken friends. Also, the words would have stuck in my throat.

I couldn't really say them out loud. I am having trouble writing this on paper, even now. Under the best of circumstances, even a night of pleasure can seem too long, but this night was interminable. All I could think of was my plan to leave the Berkshires as soon as possible and offer whatever comfort I could.

Our children were each out with their friends last night. They always try to call before the night gets going. Sometimes things get hectic and we don't reach each other, but there is always a "Happy New Year" message when we return home. As my children call me, so do Joel and I call our parents. In this way we are connected to the past and to the future, parents and children, the year behind and the year ahead.

Last night, it was good that we left early for the concert. There would not have been a cheery response to those phone calls. So this morning I had the difficult task of telling our children about the shocking and mysterious death of a contemporary with whom they had grown up.

I will leave here tomorrow. It will be a sad day – no way to say "Happy New Year." I have no happy words left, they have drowned in my sorrow for a young man who somehow lost his way.

February 21, 1999

Weekends like this make me question what we are doing in Massachusetts in February. This winter has been particularly brutal. By early January we'd had forty inches of snow in New Jersey and probably half again as much in New England. A snowy countryside is beautiful almost beyond description, but living with this beauty has its own treachery. Road conditions are a constant hazard and even thinking of going up to the country without four-wheel drive is either stupid or arrogant. The constant cold keeps me mentally shivering well past the moment I have warmed up physically. Just watching the weather report sitting in front of the fireplace can send a real chill through my body.

Despite predictions of another severe storm heading our way, this morning we picked up Joel's brother and his wife. Paul and Judy were looking forward to a couple of restful days in the country.

Joel is always delighted to show off his gadget that gets the heat pumping in the Stockbridge house. As soon as Paul and Judy climbed aboard the Jeep, Joel dialed the house from the car phone, pressing all the code buttons that would assure us of the warmth and comfort we will need about three hours from departure time. In spite of the efficiency of this wonderful invention, week in and week out, I still maintain my doubts that the thing will actually work.

The ride up the New York State Thruway was treacherous. Eighteen-wheel tractor-trailers were speeding by at about 75 m.p.h. They kicked up a tremendous amount of slush and salt, which made visibility a nightmare. The windshield wipers worked overtime. Have I been too judgmental about my friends who prefer Florida or Palm Springs? I began to question my sense of superiority about theirs being the choice of the weaker and less rugged. Perhaps theirs is the choice of the warm and the comfortable. Meantime, the choice was ours, and it was north, by choice, that we headed.

There are few "high tech" conveniences that I can appreciate, but in addition to Joel's heat switch and answering machines, I do love the cellular phone. Traveling with it ensures a sense of safety unimaginable previously. And moving along the roads towards Stockbridge, I must picture myself to be the angel of the highway, for my hand is never very far from the cellular, lest I need to dial 911 to alert the authorities about a car in distress. On this particular Friday, I called 911 so many times, it felt like I was developing a personal relationship with the dispatcher.

Poor Paul and Judy. Four not very restful hours later, we pulled into the Berkshires and settled in at the Old Mill for some wonderful comfort food and good wine. We finally reached the house, and when the door opened, we were once again warmly welcomed. It was late and we were all exhausted. After watching the late news and a final cup of tea, we couldn't wait to get under the down quilts.

Sometime in the middle of the night, I heard a dripping noise. The first thing I do when I hear anything at night is to wake Joel. "Joel, what's that dripping noise?!" "What dripping noise?" he barely replied. "It's no wonder you can't hear anything," I said. "You've been snoring so loudly it sounds like a Mack truck racing through our bedroom!"

Upon leaving our room to make a house check, I met Judy walking down the hall carrying a bucket to her room. She didn't want to wake us, but water was dripping into their bedroom and she was about to catch it with a bucket she found in the laundry room.

"So that's where the drip is." Feeling satisfied that it was being dealt with, I retreated to my bed.

It couldn't have been much later when again I heard dripping noises, but this time coming from a different place. Again it was time to investigate. This drip was very close indeed. As a matter of fact it was dripping in our bedroom. Drip drip drip. Where in the world was it coming from? I turned on the light. The ceiling was dry but the offending drip was working its way down the wall from just above the left side of the sliding glass doors that lead to the upper porch. As I trudged downstairs to get a pot to catch the water, I heard more dripping.

The house was leaking everywhere and in every room.

The dining room had two leaks. The den had water almost pouring down one wall which itself was peeling in soggy layers, some of it fallen in clumps to the floor. The downstairs guest bedroom was also dripping in two places. I didn't know if we had enough pots and buckets to deal with this. Visions of disaster danced through my head. Thoughts of possible flooding or the house coming down around us sent me running upstairs in a panic calling for Joel. From this reaction, there is an assumption that I think he could actually do something, but my need for Joel was more emotional than practical, for as great a guy as he is, handy around the house he is not.

Well, we all spent the rest of the night emptying buckets full of water into toilets and sinks all over the house.

As daylight approached, we could see how much snow had fallen in Stockbridge since we had been here a week ago. The upstairs deck showed about four feet of snow leaning up against the sliding French doors. Joel and I were grateful the house had demanded we build the porch with that very expensive load-bearing floor. Daggers of icicles hung from the roof, and the steady but slowing drip drip of melting snow continued to plague us as we ran from bucket to bucket.

At seven o'clock we called our friend and handyman Rusty. "Help! We need you now, Rusty" was my pleading cry. "How soon can you get here?" Rusty is great, and there is nothing he cannot fix. While we do not do well with anything that even resembles maintenance, Rusty gives calmness to our panic, logic to our concerns, and, most of all, his expertise to the problems that plague us.

He arrived within twenty-five minutes. "What's going on here, Rusty?" we asked, fearing the worst. "It's simple. All the gutters have been frozen solid with ice, and once you turned the heat on the underlayers of ice began to melt. Because the water had no place to go, it backed up into the house. I'll get on the roof and chop away the ice in the gutters, and that should eliminate your problem."

True to his diagnosis, Rusty soon halted the flow of dripping water by clearing the gutters. Poor Paul and Judy. The four of us spent a most unrestful morning mopping up water with bath towels and removing wet curtains that needed to be washed and replaced.

Joel and I took our guests and Rusty out for a well deserved lunch. I now look at my brother-in-law and sister-in-law with new eyes; they have moved to the head of the class in the good sportsmanship category.

The next twenty-four hours were mercifully uneventful, but you could have knocked me over with a feather when Paul asked – tongue in cheek, I am sure – just when they might join us again for another restful weekend.

April 11, 1999

In August of 1997, Susan and Michael Lerner decided to do some alterations to their country house in Monterey, a short ride from us. The house sits on a knoll at the end of a long driveway in a setting that has the illusion of being isolated but is, in fact, a quick walk to the Monterey general store and about a twenty-five minute drive to Tanglewood. It is, or was, a livable four-bedroom house that seemed to meet the Lerners' needs for twenty years. Plenty of room for the throngs of guests Michael invites all summer. As he tends to invite before checking with Susan, it is sometimes with anguished surprise that she learns of these plans; but courteous as she is, Michael's old buddies or business pals arrive to find that they are greeted with the greatest of joy – a joy that if at all forced would never appear that way to guests.

So why start messing with what seemed fine for so many years? Lately, all my friends and I have succumbed to an incurable addiction. No matter how satisfied we are with our homes, there is always one small, tiny, little itty bitty change that will make a good house into a wonderful house. As thrilled as I was when we finished this house and moved in, it was only a short time later I convinced Joel that an add-on front porch – like a small Red Lion Inn porch – would make our place more appealing. Now, four rocking chairs tell passersby that this is spot where the owners relax and watch the frenzy of cyclers, runners, and tourists moving steadily past, hoping to reach some satisfaction in their own special destination. (Of course, this is one of those fantasies. I don't think the rocking chairs have ever been burdened by the weight of bodies creaking on the rush bottoms of their slatted frames.) Then we had to add trim around the windows. The list seems to go on and on, as this quest for the perfect environment is never ending. Each change, small or large, always satisfies. Temporarily, that is. Then it is the next change that will make the house ever more fabulous. Sometimes I wonder what this search is really all about. Then my self-analysis gives way and I call my friend Jeannie to sew up new window treatments in some room or another.

The Lerners are no exception to this affliction. They decided it was time to do something minor. "We just want to enlarge our bedroom a bit and add another bathroom to the lower level guest quarters" was how they put it. The meeting with the architect went well – well for him that is, as somehow the plan had been expanded to a full-scale renovation. At this point, the job had become so large that Susan thought there was some logic to simply demolishing the existing structure and creating a new house. Michael was not in favor of this, although I think he may have had some regrets on that score as the project continues to drift on and on and on.

They were assured by the builder that construction would start in the winter of '97-98 and be finished by August of '98. The winter of '97-98 came and went, and the spring of '98 came and went, and by the promised deadline of August, the Lerners were lucky enough to have a hole in the ground, reasonably resembling the foundation for a very large den that had been added to the plan.

September moved along, but the builder was nowhere in sight. Constant calls brought no responses. Half of October had passed, and by this time the Lerners had sent letter after letter to the disappearing builder. This contractor was not returning. What happened to him we will never know. Builders can be unreliable at best and regrettably absent at worst. Horror stories of cost overruns, shoddy workmanship, and lawsuits seem to be part of improving one's house. Our friends the Kleins' new house was sagging and had to be shored up to the amount of an unplanned $20,000. Neither the architect nor the contractor would take responsibility. Our friends decided not to sue. They concluded the extra fees as well as the never ending aggravation just weren't worth the effort. And while the Kleins are now comfortably enjoying their home, Susan and Michael continue their own personal house saga.

So, in mid-October of 1998, three months after the promised completion date, a new builder was engaged to continue working on the plans. By November the house was unlivable, as so much of it was under construction. Walls had been demolished; plumbing, electric, heating, air conditioning, windows, floors, all were removed to be replaced, eventually, with everything brand new.

The Christmas season was coming with its myriad of parties and activities, and Susan and Michael were homeless. Not for long. Joel and I decided that our very dear friends could share our Berkshire home for as long as they needed. So, essentially, Michael and Susan moved in with us. They have their own key and garage door opener, in order to access the house when we aren't there. When we are together, Joel and I try to put some levity into the situation. I am finding that what we think of as levity will be more appreciated at a later time – say, in a decade or two. Maybe by then the job will be finished.

As it was with me and Joel, this project is testing the Lerners' relationship. Differences of opinion surface, and comments like Michael's "Why didn't you call the electrician about this?" or Susan's "I told you we should have torn the darn thing down!" create familiar tensions. There have been days, like this one, that Joel and I wondered if Michael would live to see another day. We are always happy to see them return to us from the construction site with Michael still in one piece.

This afternoon, when we heard the key in the door, Joel and I had stiff drinks and some cheese and crackers ready. Michael and Susan really needed those drinks. I could hear their sighs of despair over the lack of progress as they took their first sips.

We all know that this will resolve itself. Our friends will find themselves in their home one day and have years of pleasure with friends and family. The anguish and pain will diminish to be replaced by the satisfaction of a beautifully completed project. I know how they do things, and there is no doubt that we will be gasping with awe at the magnificence of their beautiful home. In the meantime, we have no idea when they'll no longer be needing our garage door opener. Joel and I can only hope, for their sake, that it is sooner rather than later.

July 17, 1999

Our guests arrived, on time, yesterday afternoon. The two couples are clients of Joel's whom I don't know very well. They are important clients and I really wanted them to feel at home. We are having typical July weather. Hot and steamy temperatures followed by pounding thunderstorms late in the day. I had planned to serve drinks and hors d'oeuvres on the porch, but nothing goes as planned, so we gathered in the living room and sank deep into the couches drinking white wine coolers that left us with a buzz long after the rain stopped. We had tickets to the Friday night concert at Tanglewood, and I began to wonder if we were going to make it as, one by one, each couple retreated to their room for a nap.

About an hour later, with a warm sun shining once again, I gently urged everyone to think about getting started. I had a picnic dinner packed and wanted to be on the Tanglewood grounds no later than 7:30 for our 8:30 concert. A lot of good cooperation and before we knew it the chairs and picnic baskets were loaded into two cars and off we went. I had a really fine time with people I'd only met once before. Sitting on the lawn eating barbequed chicken, digging into cold pasta salad, and drinking more wine, we were completely mellow. With a last lick of our messy fingers, we repacked all the empty containers and finished with a Taft Farms cherry pie. Martha, at Tafts, bakes pies that almost rival my Grandma's, and a picnic without one of her baked goodies would be an unforgivable omission.

We settled back and listened to beautiful music under the stars. Some of us were lulled to sleep and that was just fine. In other words, we were totally relaxed. That was good, because I had no idea what a day was in store for me today.

I am not the best golfer, but I do love to get out into the sunshine and play our beautiful golf course. Our company was enthusiastic about playing, and we were happy to accommodate – after all, business is business.

The men teed off first. We watched them advance down the fairway, and when they seemed far enough out, we approached the first tee. "Play it to the left side of the fairway," I said, and just then I watched Sandra take her first swing. The ball made an extreme right turn, bouncing off the cart barn and jumping out of bounds. She immediately got upset with herself. "OK," I said, "take a second shot." I was actually relieved to see her hit the ball to the left side, as suggested in the first place, even if it only went as far as a first down.

I had not realized that our guests' energetic response to my invitation to play golf could lead to such an unpleasant experience. It was a shock to find out that these women only play on an irregular basis. As this became alarmingly clear, I put on a sincere smile and committed to a good attitude, which I hoped would go a long way toward making the next four hours manageable.

The day moved as slowly as if time were mockingly standing still. Thirteen more holes, eleven more holes, nine more holes...The game crept on and on till my teeth ached with the wish that life would end soon. Throughout I gave cheerful words of praise for the better shots and solemn words of support with each wiff of the ball. I tried to fill my fellow golfers with confidence as they muttered strange sounds of agony and torment, completely blind to the fact that they only play four or five times a year.

Wow! It was almost five hours later but felt more like a month. I was hopeful that lunch was still being served at the clubhouse. I was event more hopeful that the bar was open.

We sat down and ordered drinks – mine was a large bloody Mary (heavy on the vodka, please) – and triple-decker sandwiches. Relaxing on the patio, our guests were content to gaze at the beauty of the eighteenth hole nestled beneath the Berkshire Hills, while I, gazing at the white clapboard of the clubhouse, enjoyed slurping my bloody Mary.

The round, mercifully, was over. Wishing for a swift death at one point, I didn't think I'd make it. Then came the kicker.

What? You want to play again tomorrow?! Never mind, business is business. Tonight as I write this I am feeling more like enough is enough.

September 25, 1999

I realized today that fall has finally arrived. The great summer festivals are replaced by smaller and more intimate local cultural efforts. South Mountain concerts, held for four Sundays in a superb barn building located on a deeply wooded knoll in Pittsfield, is now offering classical music performed by well known artists. The town newspapers are listing dates for jazz musicians, performance groups, theater and folk singers, all showcasing themselves in arenas such as churches and school auditoriums.

The slight sharpness in the autumn air is echoed in Joel's request to his golfing buddies that they tee it up at ten o'clock in the morning instead of half past eight. We weekenders are now visible for our long pants and turtlenecks, while the true New Englander still sports golf shorts and short-sleeved shirts.

There's an excitement, an exhilaration that pushes people to breathe in as much of the cool clean autumn air as possible. Winter is not far behind. We take the opportunities that are here and now.

It is not surprising that this combination of transient foliage seekers, part-time homeowners, and permanent residents should be treated to a number of fairs taking place weekend after weekend throughout October. They are the last hurrah for grand outdoor gatherings, as well as good moneymakers for the towns and the vendors.

The Great Barrington Taste of New England kicked off this morning. Crowds of families with young children and busloads of senior citizens seemed eager to participate in this small-town autumn ritual in which cinnamon doughnuts and fresh-pressed cider may complete a stand-up snack of Italian hot dogs or Vietnamese food purchased at one of the dozen food stands. The sounds of laughter and parents calling after their children remind me of a safer and simpler time.

A face-painting booth had kids squealing with delight, while parents and grandparents stood with pained patience for up to an hour's wait in a line that seemed to stretch for a block or more. I consider myself an indulgent grandma, but after fifteen minutes that seemed forever, I pulled Danielle, Stephanie, Geoff, and baby Matthew out of line. A mad dash to Bev's Ice Cream Shop quickly stifled the groans and whines.

Merchants couldn't have been more delighted as a sudden chilly breeze sent us scurrying into the Country Squire. I took the kids in for emergency sweatshirts, and after lots of decision-making about which color to buy, we returned home for Grandma's hot chocolate.

Next week, the Berkshire Botanical Garden will host its annual festival and the Lenox Apple Squeeze happens the following Sunday. It seems to be America's answer to the weekly marketplace that still exists in small towns all over Europe.

Yup, soon we will be bundling up, and the tourists will be gone until next spring. Joel and I, along with all the other weekenders, will leave early on Sundays to get home before the cold dark skies envelope us.

Here in New England I have become increasingly aware that the seasons of nature as well as the seasons of human life are cyclical. Perhaps that is why many older people find solace in warmer climates. The seasons don't change with such sharpness and clarity. Perhaps it convinces them that time is not passing, after all. I think something is lost in not confronting these cyclical passages. The urgency to breathe the autumn air, for soon it will be too cold, speaks to me of an urgency to examine life and live it well – and to make change or make amends now, not to wait until it is too late.

Each cycle can be dreaded or appreciated depending upon our anticipation of what is to come. I am looking forward to the next season.

October 5, 1999

We left New Jersey this morning. Six girls – at this age we actually prefer the term "girls," although I know Gloria Steinem would not approve – decided it was time to check out the Canyon Ranch Spa in Lenox. Carole asked me to join them, and, in spite of the fact that I am not a spa person, it sounded like a fun couple of days.

We signed up for a midweek group special, from Wednesday to Friday. It's a "special" because the rate is less than on the weekend and it includes one service of our choice. Because we didn't want to miss a minute of our first day, we headed up north today, Tuesday, with the idea that a day of antiquing and a night of heavy eating would gear us up for the Spartan routine that awaits us tomorrow morning.

It was an easy ride up the Palisades Parkway over the Bear Mountain Bridge to the Taconic. No traffic and acceptable weather, slightly overcast skies and a comfortable 58 degrees. Because time was not a problem, we checked out the town of Cold Spring for a little "adventure." Some words are code words, and "adventure" in this case meant shopping and spending money. We all thought that three days of boot camp exercise, food denial, and lack of shopping required pre-registration gratification.

The sun showed itself for a short time on our approach to the Bear Mountain Bridge. As we left the Palisades, a sign declared we were in Bear Mountain State Park. A quarter turn around a traffic circle, and there were the spires of a newly built tollbooth. The structure belies its utilitarian purpose, as it looks like a castle from the time of Knights of the Round Table. The spires sit on big blocks of cut stone, and the roof is slate gray although the light played with the colors as we moved closer to pay our seventy-five cents to the toll collector. The sun was dancing on the Hudson River as we crossed it. We could see for miles both south and north. Just to our left on the western side of the river sat West Point Military Academy, looking like an impenetrable fortress. A small sail-boat glided under the bridge confident that in the middle of the week it wouldn't be upended by the motorboats that speed around the river on weekends and holidays.

At the end of the bridge, the directions for Cold Spring led us north onto Route 9D – once again not to be confused with routes 9, 9W, 9E, and all those other ancillary north/south routes also labeled 9 something or another. The ride along the Hudson was lined with beautiful mansions set to take advantage of the river's view. We drove the twisting road for six miles until we spied a sign for Boscobel, an historic home open to the public. The stop at Boscobel was worth the time it took to be guided through this homestead, furnished with original pieces from the 1800s. During the summer the grounds are alive with actors playing their parts in the annual Shakespeare Festival.

The tour lasted about half an hour, and a short ride later we were parked in the town of Cold Spring. The town is very old, and its hilly streets run east/west so that from the top of the street the Hudson River is in clear view. We were greeted by lots and lots of antique stores, a fine linen shop, and a boutique featuring items from Provence. Because it was Tuesday, the usually crowded streets were empty of tourists except for six "girls" from New Jersey looking to buy anything we could get our hands on.

I immediately went into the linen store, which housed an enormous inventory of antique tablecloths and bedding. I fell for two pure white pillow shams starched so stiff their flanges were standing at attention. Not quite sure why I needed more pillow shams, but they seem to be begging me to take them out of this orphanage of linens that had been discarded by others. I couldn't begin to imagine their origin. Hyde Park, the Roosevelt family compound, was not too far away – maybe they were once on President Roosevelt's bed.

While I was doing my own thing, the rest of the group was doing theirs. Beth came away with an antique clock for her kitchen. Carole bought glazed pots from France. Leslie found bracelets that looked to me like cheap plastic, but she knew that they were very valuable pieces called something-or-another from the 1950s. I've never seen her so excited and I still can't understand why. Sandy took away a scarf of teal blue that will sway gracefully around her long elegant neck. And Yvonne found a small wire sculpture of a woman that was so delicate I feared for its safe passage back to New Jersey.

The shopping pressure was off. At the bottom of the hill was a pub with an outdoor patio, and we chose to grab some lunch. We ate disgusting things like fried onion rings and shared milk shakes, all the while not speaking about tomorrow's small portions and limited options. The train from Penn Station to Montreal runs right through Cold Spring, and as we ate next to the train tracks, the 1:50 passed us by with such force that we laughed as we held onto our French fries. Tomorrow was looming large.

The ride out of town took us east up Route 301. Once again we were winding our way up a steep narrow road that is often treacherous in winter. On our left flowed a beautiful stream and on our right were formidable cliffs. We reached the top of 301 and stopped for a few minutes to enjoy a spectacular vision. After one last twist of the road, a lake had appeared seemingly from nowhere. It was as clear and calm a body of water as I had ever seen. The lake drifted deep into the forest behind, so deep that at some point it simply vanished from sight. The left edge of the lake was bound by jagged rocks rising fifteen or twenty feet from the level of the water. The sky was a purpley periwinkle blue. There was absolute quiet. This was not the first time I had stopped at this lake. Each time I find the beauty and peacefulness almost mystical, as if angels live in the rocks protecting this environment from worldly encroachment. The girls were also awed by the sight, but I thought it better not to get into that talk about angels living in the rocks. We shared just a few minutes of quiet contemplation and someone broke the spell reminding us that we should get moving. Never mind the mystical, I thought, we are in the world of the practical and that means: get the ride over with and get back to shopping.

It took but a few minutes to reach the Taconic State Parkway. Once again we were driving north. In the rear seats Sandy and Yvonne were sleeping, in the middle seats Leslie and Beth were reading, and in the front Carole drove while I daydreamed about nothing in particular. Just under two hours later, we arrived in Great Barrington. It was four o'clock and the girls were ready for a jolt that would bring us out of the stupor we had been in. I wanted coffee and a little something to go with it, they wanted ice cream. It was easy to satisfy everyone's needs, and then the shopping began again. Funky clothes from T.P. Saddleblanket. Crystals from the store on Railroad Street for someone's grandson. Sweaters, belts, blue jeans, nightgowns, an inexpensive pearl pendant, an earthenware pitcher from Le Mistral – if it had a name, someone bought it. Tom's Toys must have had its best day in years. Each one of us grandmas couldn't resist the variety of interesting toys, games, and books. We wanted a little memory of our own trip to share with our grandchildren.

Eventually, we arrived home. The idea was for us to stay at my house so we could get to the Canyon Ranch as early as possible in the morning. It was only 5:30, but I ran upstairs so happy to see my bed that I didn't give a rat's you-know-what where anybody else slept. They were on their own. I needed a nap. Too much talk, too much shopping, too much driving, I guess too much togetherness because already everyone was on my nerves. The nap was no longer a luxury, it had become a necessity. Crankiness had set in big time.

I only took a fifteen-minute snooze and then awoke bright and cheery – not unlike a three-year-old emerging from her bed after a good ten hours of sleep. My nasty thoughts were gone, and I was eager to get downstairs and plan for the evening with everyone else.

The group had already decided on dinner. We were to bring in roast chicken and salad from the market downtown. No bread, no potatoes, maybe a diet Jell-O for dessert. It was time to get serious, after all we had spent the entire day undermining our plan to lose a few pounds and lots of dollars at the spa.

After dinner and two hours of bridge, we are now each of us in our own space. Dear journal, I am tired. I will see you tomorrow night and let you in on how the day unfolded.

October 6, 1999

I was up first as always. By six this morning I had the coffee going and was ready to exercise and diet my way from a size 8 to a size 6 in three days. With the grace of a good host, I waited until 7:30 before shouting to let everyone know that it was time to get their fat backsides out of bed.

Well, they may have been on my nerves at 5:30 last night, but this morning the five of them had clearly had enough of me. "Shut up, already" came a holler from Leslie's room. If I had let her, Leslie would have slept all morning. They came into the kitchen groggy and cranky, not at all the way I wake up. I've been told how obnoxious I am in the morning. All perky and ready for action. Some coffee and tasteless white yogurt and blueberries, and we were ready for the fat farm.

The drive to the Canyon Ranch took about ten minutes. It is magnificent. Once past the gatehouse, we drove the long winding driveway to Belle Fontaine, a marble and brick structure that has the splendor of an elaborate wedding cake. The "cottage" was built in 1897 by one Giraud Foster. The family lived grandly until Mr. Foster died in 1945, just before his ninety-fifth birthday. In 1947 Bellefontaine was acquired by a religious order. A fire in 1949 destroyed almost the entire interior of the mansion. It lay abandoned and in disrepair for many years until 1987, when Mel and Enid Zuckerman of the famed Canyon Ranch in Tucson, Arizona, rescued this grande dame and turned it into the world class spa it is today. In addition to the main house, a fully enclosed wing was added to accommodate the facilities needed to complete the spa.

The splendor of the place knocked us out. This was hardly a fat farm – it had the ambiance of a luxurious resort. We checked in and were assigned to our rooms, which are spacious and tastefully furnished in soft neutral colors with two queen-size beds. Yvonne and I are rooming together. Each of us was called for an initial consultation with a staff member at which time we each selected our free service – mine is a massage. Before long we had each individually scheduled our day. The five-mile morning walk was just my style. Ten o'clock aerobics turned out to include all of us, and then a stretch class, which had me aching an hour later.

Courtesy of The Canyon Ranch Lenox, Mass

We were hungry by then. What to expect? Low-fat, bland, small portions with limited calories and limited appeal? What a surprise! None of the above. We were seated together at a round table in the most impressive dining room with high ceilings and elaborate moldings. The menu was presented. Each item had nutritional information and the calorie count. We were free to choose from an incredible selection of foods, and we could order as much as we wanted. There was no policing us. It was up to each of us to monitor our intake of food. So far there was nothing Spartan about this experience. It was recommended that we eat lots of salad and vegetables to fill us up and consequently cut down on the need to eat large quantities of meats and starches. So we ate salad, veggies, and fruit for lunch and our afternoon snack, and lots of the above along with wonderful main courses of lamb, chicken, or fish. Dinner was served elegantly and with enough flavor to please the fussiest palate. A final apple finished off the evening after a lecture on body image.

None of us was tired, so an hour of bridge and then we were ready to sleep. Here I am, dear journal, sitting at a desk in the hall writing of the day's events so I don't interfere with Yvonne's sleep. More tomorrow.

October 7, 1999

I awoke in the middle of the night – something unpleasant was assaulting my nose. It seemed that our over-consumption of vegetables was creating some touchy moments. Too exhausted to let it bother me, I fell back into a deep sleep, mercifully removing me from the consequences of eating too much cabbage and Brussels sprouts.

When morning dawned and we were up gathering for the morning walk, Yvonne looked at me with tired, red eyes and said, “Do you know you snore?” “No, I do not!” came my defensive reply. “Oh yes, you do! I got up to go to the bathroom and I thought helicopters had surrounded the spa, but it was only you snoring. I had such trouble falling back to sleep.” “Oh yeah? Well, one of us practically blasted me out of the room, and I think it was you, so we're even,” I responded. We were like six-year-olds fighting in the schoolyard. Of course, the rest of the gang had variations on that theme in their rooms as well. Laughter and lots of it finally pulled us out of our tiredness, and from there we had our day of walking and stretching, of water aerobics and lectures on how to prepare healthy, nourishing meals. We all went a bit more lightly on the gassy foods today.

After dinner, we relaxed and then retreated to our seven o'clock massages. So another day has passed. Are we any thinner? I don't know, but what fun. What wonderful warm feelings, six good friends, sometimes spilling our poignant stories, mostly just laughing over silly things like snoring and passing gas.

October 8, 1999

I was awake at my usual six. I got dressed and went into the hall. It was eerily quiet. Was I the only person up in the entire building? With breakfast an hour and a half away, I suddenly realized I missed my own house and my own bed. It was good today was the last day. Three days without Joel is great, the fourth day becomes more than I want. So I was happy to be seeing him later after we checked out. The girls were going back to New Jersey, but Joel was driving up to the Berkshires, and I looked forward to sitting across the table from him and sharing my stories and a vodka on the rocks. I was sitting on a couch musing about seeing Joel when the rest of the group showed up and off we went for our last morning walk.

The day moved like a shooting star, gliding swiftly from morning to early afternoon. We packed our few things and feeling thoroughly virtuous left for our respective homes (mine just a few minutes away), my friends eager to hit the Woodbury discount mall on the way home to then meet husbands and go for dinner. I suspect that by the end of tonight's meal our three days of hard work will be like a body buried in cemetery – laid to rest.

My dinner was no exception. Joel and I sat by candlelight at the Inn on the Green, and my hand seemed to have a life of its own as it reached for the dark, crunchy bread lying seductively in the wicker basket. So it went, two pounds off and probably three pounds on.

November 27, 1999

As I reach some kind of maturity, it's good to know that I have developed a concrete picture of those wants and needs that will enhance my life. Our friends, also trying to label their needs, seem to be doing the same thing, now, that Joel and I did several years ago. That is, looking for a new environment to satisfy some visceral desire for change. A couple of them have gone to eastern Long Island, one to the Jersey Shore, and Yvonne and Don to Colorado.

We made our decision and looking back, the Berkshires had it all. It was accessible on a weekly basis, culture and the arts flourished year round, good food was important to us and we found no shortage of fine restaurants. Most important, we found an environment completely lacking pretension. All sizes and shapes, all manner of dress, all types of opinions seemed welcomed. I have come to understand why this area has so many facilities catering to mental health issues and personal wellbeing. There are schools for youngsters incapable of functioning in their home surroundings. There are psychotherapeutic institutes that have nurtured the rich and famous. There are yoga centers and religious camps. Even the posh Canyon Ranch Spa had found a home in the Berkshires. The spa notwithstanding, there is no flash and dash to be found here. Plain down-to-earth values generally prevail, whether at the yoga center or at the Stockbridge Golf Club. The area seems to say, "If you are high maintenance, no need to apply for residency."

Yes, this is the place for us. We are contented with our choice even though we bought a house that was a true misfit, a repudiation of all that a wonderful old country house should be. In spite of a great deal of interior renovation, our architectural style is still best called tract house motif. We often laugh that we are in no danger of being asked by the local garden club to be on its annual house and garden tour. We will never be any competition for the magnificent old "cottages" that line our street.

Walking into town this morning, I passed, as I do every day, a house that has been fascinating me since the day the contractors started to demolish the original structure. I don't know who's planning to live there, but they must be people of great wealth and even greater determination. The saga of this house continues to stimulate my curiosity.

It was shortly after we started our own renovation that the original house went up for sale. It was purchased for an exorbitant sum of money and then essentially torn down. This was the first time I had witnessed a house bought for the use of its land. The practical side of me still winces at what has now become the common practice of destroying houses instead of renovating them.

Soon the noise of the construction crews and the sight of huge bulldozers and shovels became a staple of the area. The house was going to be grand. How grand we did not even begin to imagine.

Quite spellbound, we watched from afar as the crew began tearing the house apart. Not tearing it down, but tearing it apart, always careful not to disturb the roofline. The house was dismantled until nothing stood but its frame. We had heard that the owners were required by some zoning ordinance to keep the house at a certain height, so keeping the roofline intact enabled construction to move forward.

By the time the crew had reached this point, our renovation had been completed in a record seven weeks. So we were free, as was the entire town, to concentrate on the efforts underway down the block. And concentrate we did. As we drove into Stockbridge each Friday evening, the first thing Joel and I did was ride past The House.

One day we stopped to talk with one of the construction workers and heard that The House was under the supervision of a company that usually constructs hotels and commercial buildings. He told us that the job foreman was sent to live in Stockbridge for two years, the time estimated for the completion of the project. Our curiosity continued to be piqued. Actually, everybody's curiosity was piqued for well into the summer of the following year, by which point The House barely appeared to have moved along. In fact there were carloads of workmen laboring on a daily basis. There were truckloads of materials constantly being delivered to the sight. Cement mixers and other pieces of major equipment camped out for months on end. A sculpture garden of construction apparatus seemed to be evolving.

More and more, The House became a topic of conversation. Even guests would arrive at our place and ask, "What is that fabulous structure being built down the road?" Everyone wanted to know who was building this house. The cost estimates became legendary, as into the following spring the house was still nowhere near habitable.

Architecturally, it was spectacular. A European castle was growing up right near our tract house. Fireplaces worthy of an English country manor sprouted out of the house like Jack's famous beanstalk. Windows of all sizes – round, square, oblong, and even some with leaded panes – began to grace this edifice. Oh how we longed to see the inside, but alas the entire place had been gated for some time. At night we would try to see through windows where security lights had been left to glow, but our efforts were in vain.

The summer of 1996 came and went. By fall The House, which was partially wood shingled, now sported halfway round its exterior, the most magnificent stonework I have ever seen. Incredible masonry walls snaked around the outside and up the Belgian blocked driveways. Indeed, rumor had it, that an interior elevator large enough to hold a grand piano ran up the center hallway.

In the winter of 1997, while it was apparent that one day The House would be in use, it would still be some time before somebody could call it home.

Eventually it was occupied, but we have never been in a position either to see the house or to meet the owners. More speculation surfaced – it was rumored that the owners had many such homes around the world and would therefore spend little time in Berkshire County. We contented ourselves with walking by and watching the progress of a monumental landscaping task. Before long, lush greenery would hide the house completely. And now we walk by barely aware that anything exists behind the façade of stone walls and immense evergreen trees.

We came to the country for its lack of pretension and for its understatement. I wonder if the Berkshires could ever take on the air of South Hampton. I guess not. The Hamptons would never tolerate a little tract house a few doors from its grand mansions. When I think of what is considered low key Berkshire style, I can't help but ask myself, "What's a house like that doing in a place like this?"

December 31, 1999

It constantly amazes me that the worst house disasters happen just when we are having company. I am still feeling bad about what Judy and Paul went through last February when the whole house seemed to be transported from the frigid Berkshires to a tropical rain forest, with pots catching water everyplace. Then, of course, the flood during the Tanglewood on Parade luncheon provided us with several inches of water in the basement just two hours before guests arrived. There was also the twenty-fifth anniversary party when our refrigerator decided to leave this earth on a boiling July Sunday. Carrying all the cold stuff, including a wedding cake that Nancy and I baked, to and from my neighbor's fridge added to the normal frenzy of entertaining fifty people in our home. The two of us had worked on the cake for days, carefully covering the tiers with fluffy homemade frosting that came out tough and sticky the first time and loose and runny the second time. We finally got the right consistency and then tediously decorated the cake with tiny dots of the frosting connected to each other by flowing ribbons of more frosting. As we crossed from my house to our neighbor's, we painfully watched as some of the ribbons began to bend under the summer sun until there was a path of white frosting that led from our lawn to the refrigerator in the garage next door. Then there was David's graduation party from college in late June when the air conditioning system decided to punish us by dropping dead, not to mention the dinner party when the entire house went dark as a passing storm unexpectedly came through. I don't know why our appliances turn on us. Could we be guilty of mechanical abuse? Do the machines in our house collaborate to do us dirty so many times when it is most essential that they behave themselves? What have we ever done to deserve this treatment?

Interesting that after all those breakdowns I am still hopeful enough to think that the next party will run smoothly. That's how Joel and I came to have a cocktail party for forty-five people this evening, the night before the much awaited millennium New Year's Eve. In two days we would be in another century. This called for a spectacular celebration. Music of the season sounded fabulous, so I hired a guitarist and a fiddler who would play for us the lilting sounds of Celtic ballads and folk tunes. I also hired two in help and planned a menu, with, of course, all diets in mind. The house looked great with the decorations put up for Thanksgiving still in place. I set candles everywhere, even along the walk outside. I do get charged up with anticipation. We also had two guest couples coming, and I really wanted them to meet some of our Berkshire friends.

I've heard the old cliché "Timing is everything" enough to know it is true. Never again will I have the plumber work on the well just before an event. I could have waited a couple of days, but he was available and I thought, "Grab him while you can, because these guys can be pretty elusive."

After questioning the plumber many many times about the possibilities of having trouble with the well, followed by his many many assurances that nothing could go wrong, I took him at his word. "OK, go ahead and work on the well, but it will not be a problem for tomorrow night, right?" I asked one more time. "No problem. The work will be done this morning and you'll be fine tomorrow," he replied, looking a little annoyed that I didn't have more faith in him.

By six o'clock last night, when I went to turn on the water, I knew we had a real problem. A light trickle of water was forcing its way out of the faucet, and to complicate matters, what little water was coming out was bringing sand with it. Quick, call the plumber; he was not there. I left messages everywhere, pleading messages, messages of desperation, but no response. This guy must have run away from home.

I slept very little if at all last night. I woke up every hour checking to see if the well had restored itself, and by morning there was a tiny stream of water that gave me some hope, even if it was still bringing up sand. The entire morning I spent checking faucets while Joel went to the market to buy, I have no idea how many, six-gallon jugs of water. Here we were, party day. It was supposed to be a fun day. Instead, with a growing headache I was involved in food preparation, setting up serving stations, getting the needed rentals, and doing last minute shopping because I always forget something. I began to appreciate our foremothers who hauled water from a communal well to service their household needs. There I was, hauling huge jugs of water onto the counter to cook and wash dishes.

By mid-afternoon my help arrived. These two professionals assured me that they had been confronted with some pretty peculiar working conditions and they would tackle this challenge with relish. As we worked together making caviar pies and finger sandwiches, their pleasant chatter and relaxed manner eased my sense of panic.

The afternoon went by, measured not in minutes or hours but by the number of six-gallon water containers used. By 5:30 when our house-guests arrived, Joel was calm and I was looking only slightly haggard. He took them to their rooms and offered drinks, and I was dismissed from the kitchen by our wonderful helpers. The water was beginning to recover somewhat and at least the toilets flushed. By seven o'clock we were back in a party mood. The kitchen was in capable hands, and I was dressed (un-showered, however) to receive company.

It was a wonderful night filled with good friends who can laugh with you when things don't go quite as you would like. With clapping hands and dancing to the tunes of Irish folk ballads, there was a strong sense of community. We all cried listening to the haunting melody of Danny Boy and ended the evening with forty of us holding hands singing the Scottish version of Auld Lang Syne.

Betty and Ronnie, my fabulous helpers, left around 11:30. I will be forever in their debt, as they managed to help me turn a nightmare into just a humorous calamity. I kissed everybody good night – the Wolffs, the Schactels, and my dear Joel. The house was quiet. The kind of quiet I yearned for. I sit here in the blessed stillness with just enough light to pen my thoughts on the pages before me. The fire's embers are working down to that last flicker, as I am. Can't imagine what time I will get out of bed tomorrow. Maybe not till next New Year's or even the next century.

January 7, 2000

It is so cold that, like the bears in hibernation, I am retreating increasingly into myself. I have no desire to go out or be with anyone but Joel. I am contented with coffee around the fireplace. We are enjoying light lunches, with the two of us gazing at naked branches bending under a sharp wind, listening to them crackle as one of them weakens and breaks off the tree. The days end with dinners watching a couple of movies Joel has rented from the video place downtown.

This morning I was musing, once again, about the past. What gets people to a certain place in life? I think it must be luck or lack of it. Maybe fate, yes, that is what I think. And then, of course, what each of us does with that space to which fate has guided us.

My life has been influenced by so many twists and turns of fate. I lived with Grandma and Grandpa because a particular moment in time, the end of World War II, caused a housing shortage. Being someplace a few minutes earlier or a few minutes later has probably made all the difference in the directions my life has taken. What were those moments both small and large? Who were those people who passed through my life leaving an indelible stamp in what may have been only a glimpse of time?

With a knot in my stomach I recall gym teachers who allowed team captains to choose up sides, leaving me the last pick week after week, endowing me with a dread of being judged by my peers that still makes my heart pound today. Even now, I wonder if I am a desirable partner in a golf match or if I will make that hand in a bridge game – doubts about my ability to accomplish tasks driven deep into my mind, much of it from those early passing moments in the gym. How hard I work at actually appreciating the things I can do and do well. Even concrete accomplishments never seem to erase those doubts, and sometimes I fear that friends and family will see through me and decide that I am a fraud, and then I will be picked last once again. Or even worse, not picked at all.

By some random good fortune, there were also wonderful teachers who gave me confidence and lifted me up to places I never imagined I could go. Mrs. Callendar was a rigid stickler of an English teacher who tormented other kids but somehow found purpose in encouraging me to write. "Structure, structure, and more structure" was her motto. At the end of that semester she gave me a gift – a book of poetry by Anne Morrow Lindbergh. If only I could tell her today what damage she helped undo with her extraordinary confidence in me.

Fate can move lives in all kinds of directions. One of those nuances of fate had Mother strolling along Bergen Street one spring Sunday in 1928. Dad and his friend were walking the same street. That chance encounter eventually resulted in my own chance at life. In one of those events that seem to defy logic, Joel and I came together in almost the same way. We met on a street corner in Newark, New Jersey. On a wide main street named Chancellor Avenue in an area of the city known as the Weequahic section, made famous by Phillip Roth, who also grew up in Newark.

A small city, Newark was then characterized by ethnic neighborhoods so distinct that by simply saying "Down Neck," it was understood that we were talking about the Italian section. The Weequahic section was synonymous with the Jews who had come off the boat at Ellis Island and found a home for themselves on these blocks surrounding Chancellor Avenue. There were lower middle class, two-story homes with front stoops that served as porches to sit on and watch the neighbors pass by. There were grand homes on Wilbur Avenue, where the wealthy Jews had housekeepers and fancy cars. Synagogues dotted the area every few blocks. With the understanding that there could be trouble if you strayed into areas where you did not belong, each ethnic group generally stayed and played in its own neighborhood.

Chancellor Avenue was the hub of the Weequahic section. I think that Newark in the 1950s, and in particular the Weequahic section, provided a quality of life that seems to have existed in its own time warp. This was a place where we had no fears. Knowing I was spending the night wandering up and down Chancellor Avenue, my mother never worried about my safety. Hundreds of kids just hanging around every summer's evening. Rarely, if ever, did anyone get into trouble. There were no drugs and no fights. Nothing was ever stolen. No one was ever missing. It was surely a time of innocence that generations after us have never known. A time when we could leave the key in the car, keep it running, and go into the local candy store for a Hershey bar, absolutely certain that the car would be there when we came out. It was the era of the 25-cent gallon of gas. My friends and I used to chip in a quarter a piece, and with a $1.50 spent at the pump, we could manage what little riding around we did for the better park of a week.

The junior high school and the high school were prominent on this street that, for our social purposes, ran ten blocks long. The southern boundary for us kids was the Dairy Queen, with Halem's Sweet Shoppe at the far north end. In between were a dozen different hang-outs, including the Jewish Y, where we spent nights in the summer dancing to 78 r.p.m. records. Further up the road was the Hot Dog Haven, where the hanging out was mixed boys and girls. The most famous hang-out was Syd's, also selling hot dogs and the best French fries ever to be eaten out of a greasy paper bag on overload with ketchup. Syd's, however, was a legend in its own time. Hanging out at Syd's was the sole province of the BOYS. The jocks, the fast boys, the few who smoked pot, and the very few who were on the edge of a more dangerous drug culture that hadn't yet surfaced. In other words, the boys all the girls wanted. We paraded ourselves on the other side of the street, so that the guys in front of Syd's would notice us and maybe something more would come of that.

It was a steamy July Sunday that my friend Phyllis and I were walking up Chancellor Ave. A quiet day. The empty street did not seem to have the prohibitions that were evidenced by a busy weeknight, so passing directly in front of Syd's seemed quite ordinary. On this afternoon there was no sense that we girls were trespassing on holy ground. There was only one figure standing in front of Syd's. Phyllis offered a big hello and introduced me to Joel.

Joel, handsome with curly hair and great blue eyes, standing in front of a cream and brown Chevy convertible. He wore a black shirt that made him look like a real hunk, as we said back then. My nervy friend

Phyllis had no trouble asking Joel to take us for a spin, and he, having nothing else to do, seemed eager to oblige.

A ride from Newark to South Orange in a convertible with a terrific looking guy. What a dream day. We arrived at that magic place called Grunnings on the Hill. Perhaps today it would just be another ice cream store, but then a trip to Grunnings was worth bragging about. Not only did we get treated to the best ice cream sodas ever, but the afternoon ended with Joel asking for my telephone number. I was almost paralyzed with the thrill of it all. Imagine me, a not too popular sixteen-year-old, being asked out by a Syd's guy!

That was the beginning. A young Joel, filled with enthusiasm for things I never even knew of. Classical music and theater, museums, and long rides in the country for picnics. Here was a Syd's guy, one of the bunch, a jock, but also someone interested in things most of the boys at Syd's never thought about. I was hooked. I am still hooked, and it is thirty-three years, three children, and four grandchildren later.

May 30, 2000

I can't believe I've reconnected with Carole Myers! It's been such a long time since that day we met in Singapore. Joel was going to a business meeting, and to pass the day on my own, I hopped on to a small touring van. The van had half a dozen passengers, and toward the rear was a woman who was also touring on her own. Each of us was obviously intrigued by the other. We kept making discreet eye contact and passing a comment here and there. We were the only westerners on the van and, for no other reason, this seemed to create a loose bond between us. By the time the morning was finished, our casual chattiness had escalated to intense digging into each other's lives. Really good digging required additional time, so at the tour's end we made our way to the famous Raffles Hotel for lunch.

Carole, who is English, had been widowed many years earlier. Malcolm had been the love of her life, and his long and painful bout with cancer left her alone at an early age. She told me about her wonderful daughter, son-in-law, and grandchildren. I found out that she had a home in Leeds, a two-hour train ride north of London, where her companion Neville lives in what we would call a condo but the English refer to as a flat. It was our good fortune that Neville, like Joel, was involved in business activities that morning. She had a place in Cannes, where she and Neville spent summers. On and on, we learned much about each other, me giving as much as I got. Two hours had passed, and I was sure that Joel would have concerns for my whereabouts. It was time for Carole and me to end this fortuitous meeting.

Promising to keep in touch, we parted with each other's phone numbers. Well, it's been a number of years, and three weeks ago Carole called to say that she and Neville were coming to New York. "Would you have time to see us?" she asked in her singsong British accent. "That would be a real treat," I replied and then added without even thinking, "Would you like to come to our country house over Memorial Day weekend?"

"We would love to" was the answer. I immediately felt a nauseous sensation in my stomach. I didn't even remember what she looked like. What would Joel think? Mother, as usual, would tell me I'd lost my senses for taking a strange person and her boyfriend to our home. These were the thoughts that ran through my head even as Carole and I were discussing preliminary plans for our get-together.

It turned out that Joel was delighted, and yes, Mother was almost hysterical that we could be captive to some criminal element. I still have my own doubts – after all, I have never even met Neville. What if he is demanding and unpleasant? Worse, what if he has a large mole at the bottom of his nose, and the weekend turns into an attempt to be gracious while not staring at his deformity when I am eating. In desperation I called my sister and pleaded with her and Steven to join us in this adventure or misadventure. They were not thrilled but, hearing the panic in my voice, agreed. Not only was I relieved, but Mother was happy because she felt the potential grappling with criminals would then be four against two. I kept trying to reassure Mother it was the Brits who were going to be spirited away to a remote country area with two people they didn't even know.

The plan was to pick up Carole and Neville in New York City, drive to Stockbridge, and then deposit them back at their hotel three days later. We arrived at the hotel at eleven o'clock Friday morning. I went into the lobby expecting to see a blonde woman, quite plump. Instead I heard "Gay-il, Gay-il," my name changed into two syllables with that familiar British sing-song. I turned around and to my astonishment here was a smashing brunette, very slender, and very sexy in her tight black leather pants and v-neck sweater. What was I thinking? I had absolutely no recollection of this woman, but she answered to the name Carole Myers. We embraced as if we had known each other forever. "Where is Neville?" I asked. "He'll be down in a moment." Sure enough, even as she finished her sentence, Neville joined us. Much to my relief he was quite ordinary looking, even nice looking. Not too tall, with gray hair and a pleasant smile, he kissed me hello and declared, "How very nice of you to have us to your country home." I was taken by his proper British accent, and suddenly I began to relax.

Figuring that we might show our guests the sights and pass the time having lunch and wandering around town for a bit, Joel decided to head towards Cold Spring. We were getting to know each other, and having destinations and plans was going to be important this weekend. With old friends and family, just our intimacy can sustain time spent together. Not so with people you barely know. Lots of plans, yes, lots of activities to fill what could be large, empty, uncomfortable silences. In fact, conversation moved smoothly. Neville told us that he was in the business of outfitting large yachts with fine tableware and custom designed accoutrements for the wealthiest of clients. Carole talked about their yearly trips to South Africa.

Our first true sense of connectedness came when Neville and Joel vied for the lunch check. They entered into a mock contract. In our country we would treat them and in their country they would return the favor. We all laughed and I think that was the moment we settled into a sense of comfort with each other.

Friday night Ronnie and Steven joined us, and a convivial dinner at our home was followed on Saturday with golf for the men, wandering and shopping for the women. Everybody was looking forward to the six o'clock concert – Yehuda Hanani's Close Encounters with Music. By the time we finished dinner at the Elm Court, it was understood that we were now good friends. Neville suddenly disappeared, and upon his return we discovered that he had paid the check. "What happened to our contract?" demanded Joel jovially. Just as jovially, Neville replied, "Oh, didn't I tell you? The contract expired at 8:30." What could we do but say a heartfelt thank you.

Yesterday, Sunday, we spent with lots of walking and sightseeing. My sister and her husband left for home feeling as if they had done themselves a favor as well as me. It had been a memorable couple of days. When I told Carole how Mother reacted to our invitation, she matched my story. Her daughter Corinna was quite concerned that her mother could be getting into a troubling situation. Fortunately we were all game enough to take a chance. This is about as close as I get to "living on the edge."

This morning, Memorial Day, we packed up the car and two hours later we were in front of their hotel, kissing Carole and Neville goodbye. This time, promises to stay in touch will be kept in a more timely fashion. I don't think years will go by without efforts to see each other. We are already trying to find a date to get to London.

August 8, 2000

Holy cow. It's my birthday. What happened to the dreaded F-word? Has it really been ten years since I turned fifty? There are times I feel twenty and times I feel my age, which is hard to actually put on this page.

Once I came to terms with fifty, I began to manage things quite well. Gray hairs – not a problem. A one-process job in the beauty salon and there I was, not a gray hair in sight. A few lines in my face – not a problem. A little injection of the latest wrinkle-smoother from the dermatologist and amazingly the lines were gone. A hot flash here and there – not a problem. A prescription from the gynecologist, and before you know it, I had the left the sweats behind. No more taking that nightgown off and putting it on, over and over, as if some alien force had invaded my body and caused my very own hormones to turn on me. Well, it's a decade later. In the mirror this morning, I saw deeper lines, slightly sagging jowls, and – worst of all – my neck beginning to hang in folds like the un-ironed creases of a linen tablecloth. A strapless dress reveals a bulge of fat hanging over the back of my gown, and my arms seem to have sprouted extra skin that sways back and forth at the touch of my hand. There are five extra pounds that, as hard as I try, seem to have become a permanent part of my anatomy. How will I come to terms with all that? It seems that everything has increased but my energy level.

I try to tap into the best that surrounds me. In ten years, since Danielle was born, we have added five new grandchildren. The most recent – Mark and Lara's son Justin – born in May. Today we offered to baby sit, and along with being one of life's true blessings, it was also a blast of reality.

This afternoon Mark and Lara left our little Justin with me and Joel so they could have a couple of hours to themselves. Our little guy is three months old. So sweet, so good. We were thrilled to have him.

His parents blew kisses goodbye and off they went. Suddenly, our little angel became a howling prince. He cried and cried, ceasing his piercing screams only if we carried him in our arms and walked him around the yard. The second Joel or I stopped walking, the crying started again. I think we must have walked four miles. Our little bundle of joy became heavier and heavier. Joel and I began tossing him back and forth every few minutes like a football moving towards a first down.

We remembered the anguished cries of our own small babies and our attempts to calm them. Nothing worked then and nothing was working now, except for meeting Justin's demand that we keep walking him round and round the yard. He finally settled down when he was good and ready, about an hour and a half later. A bottle of milk and he was fast asleep. A bottle of wine and so were we.

Eventually, when Mark and Lara arrived, they wanted to know how everything went. "Just great," we lied. "We had a wonderful time," adding silently in our minds, "and now you can have him back."

It is true that one of the big pluses about being grandparents, unlike parents, is that you can give the little ones back. It is our joy to have Danielle, Stephanie, Geoff, Matt, and now Justin come to visit with us. It is also our joy to return them to their parents, as it seems caring for them takes considerably more energy and patience than we have. Not unlike my face, which also takes considerably more energy and patience, not too mention cosmetics, to try to look almost as good as it used to. We are exhausted. Why is that? Simple really. Because sixty is even older than fifty.

September 12, 2000

Yes, sixty is beautiful. My daughters-in-law and daughter gave me a birthday party to remember. Sometime in June we had talked about such a celebration to be held at Nancy's home but decided to wait until early September since so many of my friends are away in the summer. This has been the story of my birthday life, never being able to celebrate because I was born while everyone seemed to be someplace else.

I was happy to be involved in the party planning. I never did like surprises. Maybe it's my control impulse, but I want to create my own guest list. When I turned forty, my family graciously surprised me and I suddenly found myself looking around wondering why this person was there, and worse, why someone who should have been there had not been included. I didn't mind the addition of the unexpected guests but felt so uncomfortable that someone who belonged had been inadvertently left out.

Not only was I in complete charge of the list, but I was firm in not wanting any gifts. Knowing my friends and family are too generous to abide by this request, I decided that we could put their generosity to good use. Acting on my behalf, my good friend Lynda was the perfect conduit. She had Jewish Family Service set up a self-liquidating fund, which was temporarily to be called the Gayle Fund. Monies deposited as a result of my birthday party would be used to ease the lives of a single mother in need of support. This fund would be available to all, as Jewish Family Services in Union County, New Jersey, is a non-sectarian agency. This was exactly what I wanted.

Lynda spread the word, and at the end of today's delayed birthday festivities, the Gayle Fund has a substantial amount of money that will benefit a deserving recipient. I am hopeful that this money will enable a woman to lift herself and her children out of a difficult situation and get her "back on her feet."

So this afternoon was a success in many ways. My caring girls hosting so many friends with a luscious tea party. A day of feminine declaration. Dainty tea sandwiches, scones, jams, and heavy whipped cream set on lacy paper doilies. Tea pots and delicate china cups and saucers set up on small folding tables – all creating the feel of a ladies' tea room. Beautiful tributes from close friends and a lovely poem from granddaughters Danielle and Stephanie. A day for women – for those of us fortunate enough to be able to manage life dotted with those "champagne problems" and, I hope, a day for one woman, not so fortunate, who, with the help of our Gayle Fund, may manage her life with a little more ease and a lot more hope.

October 22, 2000

When the weather is not ideal and guests are going to arrive, we often try to find some options for an afternoon's activity. A massage and lunch at the plush Mepal Spa can be a fabulous way to pass a dreary day in the Berkshires. A trip to the Clark Museum in Williamstown is always a winner. And of course the movies are an option. When none of these will do, the guys are usually happy watching endless ballgames which invariably end up in a general nap time. There is nothing sexier than three or four men laying on chairs or couches, heads slouching every which way, the foghorn sounds of snoring emanating from their collective noses.

The wives, on the other hand, are usually ready to leap into an antiquing frenzy. Sometimes their zeal can only be compared to fillies ready to snap out of the gate at Churchill Downs. The antiques stores and art galleries are so extraordinary that I don't mind going into some of them time and again. I have my route of the-best-of-the-best and never tire of filling my eyes with the superb and sometimes rare items found in these places.

The Country Dining Room in Great Barrington always has me lost in fantasy, imagining the elegant dinner parties that fashionable society held in their Berkshire "cottages" long ago. Dining tables of polished mahogany, upholstered chairs with beautiful beading and needlepoint seats, gorgeous sideboards and trolleys, cut glass epergnes, and fantastic candelabras. Everything one needs or wants to create an extra-special dining experience is located in this shop just minutes from our house. This is the first stop on my tour for our guests.

Continuing further into downtown Great Barrington, we often stop at Le Mistral, a store dedicated to all things beautiful from France – Provence in particular. This store carries an enticing array of cutlery, dishes, and French country photographs. It is an irresistible place for casual wandering.

We then move down Route 7, passing a collection of antique stores and galleries that line both sides of the road for miles, and always try to wind up at the Loring Gallery around 12:30. This is not by accident, as it is lunchtime at the gallery. Each day the proprietors, Anne, Natalie, and Rosemary, set out a feast for those smart enough to be around the gallery at that time. Lunch is satisfying, but it is the art that is fabulous. These women have an eye for what will please. Everything they select – from the soft and soothing to the often cutting-edge – pleases me. I manage to buy at least one piece every year, and if budget and wall space were not considerations, I would certainly own more.

My guests invariably find something to take home with them. From the Country Dining Room, it is often candleholders or napkins rings or an occasional pearl-handled carving knife. From Le Mistral, perhaps a piece of French earthenware from Mustier, and from the Gallery maybe a small whimsical piece of wall art. These tend to be tokens – not inexpensive, but reasonable items that can be carried home.

This weekend, however, the economy in Berkshire County was turned upside down by one of my guests, at least for a day.

This was expected to be a very dreary October weekend. Florida was about to get pummeled by another hurricane, and rain from the last storm was just working its way through the Berkshires. Two couples arrived Friday afternoon. The rain was so fierce that we canceled our reservations, deciding that dinner at home was the logical choice. We sat around listening to the wind howl like wolves in search of prey, and that lead to a discussion of Saturday's options. All suggestions were rejected. The guys figured they would spend the day lazing in front of the TV watching football.

Saturday morning after the men confirmed that they had nothing but TV in mind, the women, not surprisingly, enthusiastically wanted to shop the wonderful stores on Route 7, so on the tour we went. I foresaw a day of browsing with a bit of casual buying thrown in. Wow, was I wrong. Jessica had serious business in mind, and Route 7 was about to have a stupendous weekend.

First stop, the Country Dining Room. "I'm looking for a dining room table and chairs for our home in Florida," Jessica said to Mike Chavetz. "What do you have in mind?" he asked. She was quick to reply, "I know just what I want, an antique round table that will open up with two leaves." "Round tables were not ordinarily made with two leaves a century ago, but I happen to have such a rare piece on the floor," replied Mike. We all went to see this rare table, and it was a beauty – polished mahogany with a rim of inlaid cherry that indeed opened up to receive two leaves that would seat twelve people comfortably. Jessica was thrilled. "What type of chairs would you suggest?" she asked. Well, two hours later, she had selected the table, six chairs that once belonged to an ambassador, and a magnificent sideboard. With a total price tag exceeding $20,000, Jessica took a backward step and said, "Let me think about this for a while and bring my husband back later."

Back in the car I suggested we might try a few more antique stores. It made sense to explore what other dealers had to offer. Our drive south on Route 7 took us into Paul Kleinwald Antiques and then to the Trianon, both of these shops selling the finest of old furniture, but at that moment they had nothing that interested Jessica. We finally ended up at Susan Silver Antiques, whose fine antiques rival anything we could ever find in the prestigious New York and Palm Beach shows. The shopkeeper echoed Mike Chavetz's words when she told us that round tables with two leaves were exceptional, and she did not have one. However, an old French chandelier with amethyst crystal drops caught Jessica's eye. We all agreed it was magnificent. Discussion on price ensued, and once again she decided to give it some thought.

It was 12:30 and what a coincidence – down the road was the Loring Gallery. We popped in for lunch and for what I thought was a casual browse. I should have known better by now. This gal was really serious, and before you could blink, Jessica and gallery owner Anne Schnessel were talking about a wonderful painting that I have coveted since it was hung in the late spring. The subject is a woman lying in a dressing gown on a luxurious chaise lounge. It is painted in shades of scarlet and soft yellow and evokes an image of pampered aristocracy. Leaving Jessica and Anne to discuss the artwork, Lana, our other guest, and I heaped our plates with one of Natalie's abundant spreads and found ourselves talking with an artist who had come to the gallery on business. Not long after lunch, we returned home with Jessica, who was thinking about the Charles Apt painting also.

We arrived at the house to find three napping men. My first comment to Jessica's husband was "You would have been smart to have gone to the spa or a museum today. Your wife may have beefed up the entire monetary structure of Berkshire County all by herself." After the color came back into his face, Stuart listened to Jessica talk about all the pieces she had seen. She was very much on edge, and Stuart was quite shocked. Their tension was apparent. "Should we or shouldn't we?" "Will everything arrive in Florida in good condition?" "Are the pieces worth the price?" "Will thy actually work in the room?" All legitimate questions when spending large sums of money on furniture and art that needs to be shipped and set up 1,800 miles from here. Somewhat recovered and with good humor, Stuart agreed to see all that Jessica had found.

The shops open at eleven on Sundays, so this morning after breakfast a very nervous Jessica and her husband took a return trip to all three shops. They spent the better part of today assuring themselves that the pieces were perfect, that the prices were realistic, and that everything would be shipped by carriers specializing in antiques. They asked for and received detailed history on the items they were about to purchase, and Jessica seemed thrilled that her Florida dining room would be complete. The day was proving profitable for all.

Jessica and Stuart came back to the house with much enthusiasm. They were keyed up with emotion but still slightly on edge by what they had done so unexpectedly.

By this time I was a nervous wreck. So much agitation and worry on my part, hoping our guests would be happy with their purchases as if somehow their lasting pleasure was my responsibility. Yes, it surely was time for a drink. No wine for me, I needed a large vodka straight up to calm my queasy stomach.

Our company left at about five o'clock. They returned to New Jersey and all was calm, but only for the time it took for them to arrive at their own homes. At about nine the phone rang – it was Jessica on the other end. Last minute jitters were giving them second thoughts, she told me. "We are worried about the size of the table and concerned about whether the chandelier is right for the room. Now that we have paid for everything and arranged for shipping, Stuart thinks it makes sense for us not to make this commitment right now. Also, I feel we are spending more than we should. I think I got carried away too quickly," she added. Nausea crept into my belly, for I could certainly relate to their feelings. Every time I buy something I wonder if it is right. I even find committing to theater tickets gets me wired as I worry that something will go wrong on that date and we might be left with expensive tickets. "I feel so terrible about all of this confusion," she added, "but we are concerned about whether our money will be refunded now that the transactions were completed." "I understand your feelings. You are making the right decision if you have doubts, after all these pieces are with you for a lifetime and you need to be absolutely certain. I am sure that these reputable shops will refund your money without question," I said, hoping to instill some comfort into an uncomfortable situation. We agreed that first thing tomorrow morning Jessica would need to make some phone calls. I hope I am right that the shops' owners will be amenable to the requested refunds.

October 23, 2000

I barley slept, I was so very upset about the idea that we had guests who went home agitated instead of relaxed. Jessica and Stuart are two of the world's finest people, generous philanthropists and the type of friends who would do anything they could to make someone else's life better. I didn't want them to feel uncomfortable, and so naturally I took on their feelings and was up all night worrying about the situation.

Jessica called me at eleven this morning with relief in her voice. She had called the Country Dining Room to cancel the table and was keeping the chairs and the sideboard. Concerned about the size of the table, she would continue searching for something more suitable. Sheila Chavetz was kind and gracious, agreeable to any changes that Jessica wished to make. Jessica also called Susan Silver and left a message that she had decided to hold off on the chandelier at this time but was still thinking it over.

Jessica had taken the painting from the Loring Gallery home and had hung it over the fireplace in her living room. Both she and Stuart felt it was exactly right for their New Jersey residence. They are eager to get to Florida early next month to receive the pieces that are now in the process of being packed and shipped. Everybody seems to have profited.

However, I don't know if I can ever go through this again. Next time when friends want to go antiquing, I will vette their intentions. Serious or casual? If the answer is serious, my response will be "Go visit somebody else."

January 4, 2003

Sorry, dear journal. I have ignored you for a long time. It's been more than two years. Sometimes life intrudes on life, some intrusions are sad and some are joyous.

David got a fabulous job in Washington D.C. He, Mindy, and the boys moved to Fairfax, Virginia, which is a big adjustment for me, as I always enjoyed knowing that they were only twelve minutes away. They had lived next door to Mark and Lara, a situation which, in today's world, is quite unique. They are very happy in D.C., though, and in the end that's all that matters.

Last May, Mark and Lara added joy to our family. Sloane was born on the 28th of the month, the same day her brother Justin was born, several years before. Time is passing by at an alarming rate. Has it really been twelve years since we first rented in Stockbridge? The holiday season passed by so swiftly it felt like all the moments were crunched together in one short blur. Beginning with the family descending for Thanksgiving weekend through the planning for another New Year's Eve, the last month and a half were filled with constant activity. A sadder season to be sure, because Dad left us this past fall. At ninety-one he was as clear thinking as any young man. My Daddy, who made sure that I had braces on my teeth, who took me with him Sunday mornings when he went bowling with the league. On our way to the bowling alley, we always stopped for pancakes at the Tuttle House, a tiny restaurant with a counter and a few stools. When we lived with Grandma and Grandpa so many years ago, every night Dad read me a story before bed. He then put a clean handkerchief under my pillow in case I sneezed at night (allergies plague me to this day). Dad was a great golfer, and he must have had high hopes for me as he took me to Weequahic Park for lessons with the pro. This was a big sacrifice – money was always scarce, and he managed not only to pay for the lessons but to make time to get me to the golf course. Although he never would say so, I am sure he would have liked it if I had become good at the game. In spite of the fact that I am at best a mediocre athlete, I still play golf a couple of times a week.

In the last two years, Dad had become more and more frail. It seems that the loss of his youngest brother was a catalyst for the rapid failure in his health. He was never in pain and never complained, but he was so weak that he needed a cane for support. The closest he got to expressing discouragement was when I picked him up for lunch one day and asked him how he was doing. "I'm struggling, hon," he answered. And I saw his own sense of uselessness and embarrassment because he was no longer the robust man of just a few years before.

When a fall resulted in a paralyzing stroke, Ronnie and I began to pray for the end. Our Daddy in a hospital bed, garbling his words, frustration on his face with every anguished effort to make himself understood – this was too painful to see. Yet every day for two weeks we watched, sometimes with Mother, sometimes with my cousins Billy and Bobby, whom my father adored as if they were his sons. His young friend Kenny also sat with us almost daily and watched as Daddy drifted moment by moment towards his last moment. Finally he was at peace.

Almost a month later, even with a constant sadness, I did what I normally do to prepare for the holiday ahead. Down to the basement to haul up the big plastic bags holding the treasures accumulated from seasons past. The garlands were wrapped around the banisters going upstairs to the bedrooms and downstairs to the playroom. Glass berries were affixed to the garlands and so were the twigs tied together with ribbon that Danielle and Stephanie had made the year before. Candles lined the staircase and at night cast a glow through the whole house. The mantle also got much consideration, with more garlands and snowmen that sing holiday songs when their tummies are pressed by little grandchildren. The Wizard of Oz was in evidence with Dorothy, Tin Man, Cowardly Lion, and Scarecrow dolls lining the mantel. In the center of the mantel, I always place a Chanukah menorah handmade by Geoffrey. He probably felt we needed a reminder that we are Jewish, as he once looked at the decorations around the house and asked, "Grandma, aren't you Jewish like us?" Since my parents never objected to Ronnie and me hanging our stockings at Christmastime, I guess doing some minor decorating always felt quite natural.

The Wednesday before Thanksgiving, our kids, grandkids, Ronnie and Steven and their children and grandchildren, as well as Mother arrived here. We had dinner, told stories about Dad, and then all of us bedded down on every available cot and sleep sofa in the house.

Thanksgiving morning brought our neighbors up the hill to make the candy houses that have been a tradition since our children were young. Bagels for the adults; lots of chocolate, frosting, and marshmallows for the kids. By noon, we had cleaned the kitchen and the noise had diminished somewhat. We had Thanksgiving dinner at the Elm Court, which was Nancy's excellent idea. No cleaning up. Yes. That was good.

On Friday morning the first wave of guests departed. My sister's family threw kisses goodbye. Mother also headed back to New Jersey with them. We had endured the first holiday without Dad. It wasn't easy, but life doesn't always offer a choice, so even with pain in our hearts we spent this holiday thankful that Dad didn't suffer very long and we had each other to share our grief.

The weekend ahead of us and our family, Joel and I decided it would be fun for our children and their spouses to spend the day at a spa. The Canyon Ranch is fabulous but will only accommodate resident guests, so Cranwell Hotel and Resort with its new world class spa and fitness center was the logical choice. David and Mindy, Nancy and Neal, and Mark and Lara jumped on the idea of an afternoon of relaxation without any kids. As for Joel and me, we were just as happy to stay at home with the six grandchildren.

When everyone returned looking so calm I thought they were comatose, Joel and I needed our own space. We headed to the Norman Rockwell Museum, which was host to the autumn's first Close Encounters with Music concert of the year. After a busy three days and nights, nothing could have soothed us more. Joel and I returned home refreshed.

On Sunday, carload by carload, our kids and their kids departed until we were enveloped in a dense but comforting quiet.

We lit Chanukah candles a few weeks later. Soon after, the sounds of

Christmas music took over the airways. Christmas specials on television were a welcomed change from the grim fare that currently poses as drama these days, and the inns and restaurants were decked out with festive decorations.

Here we are, 2003. Another year. What will the coming months bring?

February 12, 2003

What a brutal couple of months. We returned this morning from ten days in palm tree paradise – Boca Raton, Florida. For ten days we were relieved of the miserable cold that has been gripping the Northeast for the last six weeks. Five days with Myra and Alan and five days with Yvonne and Don started us thinking about a small condo for ourselves.

Even though the temperatures were warm, there were two rainy days. What do you do in Florida when it rains? Current homeowners go looking for an upgrade, and those of us just visiting spend a rainy day with a realtor hoping to find the fantasy space that is just perfect for as little money as possible.

Bingo. Judy Romanow, recommended to us by both hosts, couldn't have been happier we called. I swear, by the time we hung up the phone, Judy was knocking at the door with a bunch of listings in the same community as our friends.

Tension between Joel and me mounted. Were we ready to own a third residence? What kind of time would we spend in Florida? What would our expenses look like? What would my mother say?

With no other plan on tap and no let up in the weather, we let Judy do her thing. "We want a minimal commitment," Joel said. "I agree. We don't need a house, just a small condo, something to go to for a few days' relief from the winter's cold," I chimed in. "I have plenty of time and if you are game, we can look at seven residences on the market, all meeting your needs," said Judy. Wow, that Judy is smart.

Some units had no view, some were dirty, some were in need of extensive repair, some were overpriced, but finally we came to the perfect spot. A two-bedroom, two-bathroom condo with a great screened-in wrap-around porch and beautiful views from every room in the place. The unit was owned by a British couple who had not returned to Boca this past winter and were hoping to sell as quickly as possible. The unit is a turnkey, which means that it is fully furnished and ready to be lived in on the day of the closing. It was really priced to sell, and after days of negotiating by fax, we signed on the dotted line, knowing that we had three days to change our minds.

My heart was pounding. Are we nuts? Two little kids from New Jersey who started out with nothing. Yes, then there is my mother and Joel's father. They are from the "old school." That means their first response is to object ferociously. Object to what? Object to everything, especially those things that require money and anything that looks like too much luxury. Even though we are wholly independent, never ask for a cent, somehow our parents feel comfortable – no, feel obligated – to warn us about the dangers of spending too much or living the "good life." "What do you need it for?" is one of my mother's favorite expressions. "Can you afford it?" is another. And finally, "You'll wear yourself out." Still not sure what this last one means, even though I have been hearing it all my life. Joel's father can't even accept the idea that we wanted to leave our car in the airport's long term parking for a week. "Spend money on parking?" he barked and insisted that he drive us instead. This meant Dad had to be at our house at six in the morning for us to catch an eight o'clock plane. No amount of pleading would change his mind. In addition to our own misgivings, we also will have to struggle through our parents' determination to "talk some sense into our heads."

We considered for another day. Can we really do this? Eventually, after endless discussions, Joel and I decided this condo would be ideal. Even if we use it on a limited basis, our kids can enjoy it as well. And with all those precious little grandchildren, it seems like a good idea for the whole family. Looking at the numbers on paper, we were beginning to feel confident.

We returned to the condo one more time to make sure that it was for us. The place was perfect, but it didn't seem like a good time to mention to Joel that the every room needed to be refurnished. My friend Brenda once said that turnkey actually means you turn the key and then throw everything out. That is an appealing idea, but I think we will live with what is there, at least for a while.

We are back in the Berkshires, once more, and to tell the truth, it seems a little less cold up here now.

March 24, 2003

During the last few weeks Joel and I have been talking about putting the house up for sale. We are both conflicted, but after seven years we feel that we cannot maintain both the house and the New Jersey golf club. We have agonized over this decision, but our choice is to stay in New Jersey. Buying the condo in Florida last month really pushed our decision. Joel and I both feel that three residences will be more of a burden than a blessing. Finances aside, every weekend in the spring and fall, the turmoil about whether to drive north or stay in New Jersey has caused us more angst than pleasure. With our six grandchildren, two of whom are now in Virginia, the need to be with family and not such a distance away also figures into our decision.

So today we put our lovely Berkshire hide-a-way on the market. Mole and Mole are our realtors, and already they have clients to bring over to the house.

The sign will go up tomorrow on our front lawn. I am anticipating all the questions from friends and neighbors about our choice to leave Stockbridge. We've bought and sold enough houses to know that the questions never end. It becomes annoying to meet people in the market or at the golf course – whether they know you well or not, they feel the need to ask if the house sold. What is it their business? How does it help them or me to have to talk about this sale? I guess I am more agitated than I realized. I think I will feel better once we actually sign the final papers and begin to live full time in New Jersey.

That's it. I can't think about this another minute.

May 18, 2003

We've had a lot of lookers at the house but no buyers. David, Mindy, and the boys spent the weekend with us, and the boys were very unhappy to hear we were selling.

We were out so late last night that when we arrived home we did not check the answering machine. At nine this morning, Tiffany, the realtor, called to remind us she had left a message about bringing prospective buyers to see the house at 9:20. "What?" I screamed. "Everyone is still sleeping and the house is a mess." "I will stall them till 9:45 or 10:00 if I can," she said. "I can manage that," and then I became a whirling dervish. "Get up, get up, make your beds, and clean the rooms. Straighten the bathrooms and make sure the wet towels are in the hamper." I gave one order after another, trying to get the place in shape for the hopeful home-buyers coming at any moment.

Mindy set the table on the porch. We had a beautiful sunny morning. We sat down. Pancakes, bacon, and eggs were in the skillets. Bowls of berries were on the farm table. What an appealing scene was set. We all sat "calmly" down for breakfast when the door bell rang. "Good morning," I said as Tiffany introduced me to a handsome young couple. "Please come in and look around," I continued as if life had been peaceful and serene all morning.

They walked in the door and suddenly grandson Matthew appeared looking annoyed. Our little guy started grilling these lovely people. "Who are you and what are your names?" our little guy demanded. David quickly ushered him back to the porch.

There we were, Mindy and David facing the sun-drenched mountains, Joel and I facing the clapboard house, and the boys having a great time running around the porch. A seductive scene. By lunchtime we had an offer, which we refused. By late afternoon we had a higher offer, which we refused. By dinnertime the next offer was in our ballpark and a deal was made.

Our buyer had just one more question: "Would we be willing to sell the house furnished?" "I will be happy to leave everything but the clothes in the closet," replied an eager Joel. "Let me see the clothes in your closet," joked the buyer. And that was that.

We are to close on the house in three weeks, as the buyers would like to use it this coming season. That old cliché "sometimes you get what you asked for" – I think that's what happened to us today. It is definitely the right move to sell the house, but I know that I am in for another sleepless night.

June 17, 2003

This morning we had our closing. Once again conflicting feelings settled in. Confusion about whether we had done the right thing clouded my sense of relief about not having to run up to the country every weekend. Joel and I had discussed it long enough for me to know that it is the right move at this time. After all, life will be calmer without worrying that pipes might freeze in winter or the well could suddenly bring up sand in the summer. We will be relieved of all those additional expenses that come with home ownership.

The couple that purchased the house obviously had no such conflicts. The joy and anticipation on their faces was in contrast to my own doubts, but there we were in the attorney's office and the deal was firm. We signed the papers and turned our Berkshire retreat over to its new owners. The buyers had bought it fully furnished. We even left our soda, beer, and wine for them. All they needed to do was to open the front door and retreat to the porch for what may be one of the rare times they get to gaze at the mountains. One weekend, the new owners will entertain their first set of friends, and as they sip drinks on that porch one of them may suddenly realize that having guests means never seeing the view.

So we left the Berkshires for a final time, and now I write about this last moment here at the kitchen table in New Jersey. It is late afternoon and we are having dinner with all the kids and grandkids at Nancy's. This is what I wanted, and as I look forward to kissing all of those beautiful faces, this morning's doubts are already receding in my mind.

Afterword

May 2, 2005

Two years have gone by. New Jersey has been all I had expected when we sold the Stockbridge house. Our lives have been free of the champagne problem of wondering what to do with ourselves each weekend.

But about six weeks ago, Joel and I suddenly missed the weekly rides. We even became nostalgic about the process of piling up the car with items that we are sure cannot be had in Berkshire County. What about Tanglewood and the Berkshire Theatre Festival? We hardly saw the Elm Court crowd these past couple of years, although we have all tried to keep in touch. We began to long for our old summers in the Berkshires, and Bob Kohn was having a fit that he had no place to stay for Tanglewood on Parade. He and Sonny even went so far as to book a bed and breakfast, but he did not let us forget that he missed our B&B. Our grandchildren complain that they do not have a big porch to chase each other on and ask why we did such a terrible thing as to leave them without a fun place to visit. And with another grandchild, three-month-old Todd Harris, having joined the family, Joel and I began thinking about the possibility of another home in the Berkshires.

It didn't take long before we called Charlotte Gross and started to hunt for the right house in the right place. We found it sooner than expected and we close in two weeks.

Of course, we'll have to renovate.

Appendix

Gayle's Guide to the Berkshires

This Appendix offers a partial list of what is available to you in this geographic region that I love so much. I have visited most – but not all – of the restaurants, hotels, music halls, and other venues that I write about here (starting in southern Berkshire County and moving toward northern Berkshire County). I felt it necessary to include a somewhat broader list than my experience would allow, especially in the area of lodging, to give you a wider choice of price, ambiance, and location. Current information is available at the websites listed.

For the most up-to-date activities in Berkshire County, log on to www.BerkshireEagle.com and click on Berkshires Week. It always enhances a trip to know in advance how to make the most of your stay.

Have a fabulous time!

Gayle Harmelin

LODGING

Before the rental house, we managed to stay at many inns, B&Bs, and hotels in the area. During our renovations, once again we found lodging in a number of the places listed below. Unlike the B&B we first stayed at, which was a huge disappointment and no longer exists, the following establishments should offer fine accommodations. Don't forget, rates will often determine the level of amenities, so choose according to your needs – economy or luxury.

New Marlboro

Gedney Farm and Mepal Manor – Route 57

Formerly a cattle barn, Gedney Farm was fully renovated to house sixteen unique suites, some with fireplaces. The one-time horse barn, located opposite the lodgings, is an interesting venue for weddings and parties.

Joel and I spent the night at the Farm quite a long time ago and found the unusual design of the interior spaces architecturally appealing. Many years later, our friends held their daughter's wedding in the old horse barn, and it was a smashing success. In this day of cookie-cutter affairs, the wedding came off as quite special. Room rates run about $250. Innkeepers Brad and Leslie also own Mepal Manor, which is a true manor house built in 1902. The rooms are newly renovated and decorated, and the bathrooms keep that old-world flavor without the old-world stodginess. An adjacent building erected two years ago, when the Mepal Manor property was purchased, houses a spa offering numerous services. We have had massages there a number of times, and, at our request, we have followed our spa experience with a sumptuous lunch at the manor house. Room rates are about $100 higher than at the Gedney Farm sister property. See www.GedneyFarm.com or call 800-286-3139.

The Old Inn on the Green – Route 57

The Old Inn will be described below for its exceptional restaurant; but above the restaurant are four rooms, and just across the driveway the Thayer House offers six additional rooms. I have never seen the rooms, so I can't speak from experience, but the website has a picture and description of each room along with the rates. See www.OldInn.com or call 413-229-7924.

Egremont

The Egremont Inn – Sheffield Road

Twenty rooms are available at very reasonable rates. Egremont is a small village; and stepping out of the Inn, you can walk to a couple of antique stores, a rare books store, and the best ski shop in southern Berkshire County. A small queen-bedded room lets for about $135 per night in season. Worth looking at. See www.EgremontInn.com or call 413-528-2111.

Great Barrington

Christine's Bed and Breakfast – Route 41

I pass this B&B every morning on my two-mile walk. I stopped to chat with Christine one day and found a gracious lady, enthusiastic about her establishment. Four rooms decorated in warm florals, each with private bath, and a glassed-in breakfast area. Guests are treated to afternoon cocktails on the flagstone patio. Christine will provide afternoon tea, if reserved in advance. If you are looking to stay in a B&B that feels like a visit with friends, check out this one. See www.ChristinesInn.com or call 800-536-1186.

The Holiday Inn Express – Route 7

No surprises here, as this Holiday Inn is consistent with all of the newer type of motels currently being built. It is a relatively new establishment. The rooms are appointed in the usual inoffensive motel motif. My elderly parents stayed here and were treated with great care. The staff is courteous, the place is clean, the breakfast room is inviting with a fireplace and glass windows overlooking a meadow. It also boasts an indoor pool and a fitness center. See www.HolidayInnExpress.com. For direct access to the Inn call 413-528-1186.

Stockbridge

The Red Lion Inn – Main Street

This is an old hotel. The rooms are small, furnished in an old-fashioned country look. In addition to the main hotel, there are a number small guest houses around town and these may have additional amenities. All are immaculate, the service is excellent, and a stay at the Inn is the quintessential New England experience. It is perfectly located. You can take in the charming town of Stockbridge just by walking out the front door of the Inn. There are restaurants in the area, and the Berkshire Theatre Festival is a ten-minute walk down Main Street. Room rates vary widely according to season and type of room. See www.RedLionInn.com or call 413-298-5545.

Wheatleigh – Hawthorne Road

A magnificent Italian Palazzo that was once one of the Berkshire "cottages,"

Wheatleigh is an experience in luxury. This is one of the numerous places Joel and I stayed long before we had thoughts of actually renting in the Berkshires. The entry hall décor is stark modern, a sharp contrast to the old-world architecture of the building itself. We go to Wheatleigh occasionally for brunch, and there seems to be a general coldness about the place although the staff is certainly pleasant and attentive. Large rooms, attractively furnished, many with fireplaces and some with balconies. I remember, many years ago, opening the French doors in the evening and being treated to glorious music floating across the road from nearby Tanglewood. If you book in advance, try to avoid one of the ground floor rooms facing the front of the hotel. It can feel uncomfortably visible from the circular driveway. The hotel boasts a world-class restaurant, a beautiful outdoor pool, and a lovely terrace. It is very pricey with some rooms fetching up to $1,500 a night. See www.Wheatleigh.com or call 413-637-0610.

The Inn at Stockbridge – Route 7

We have never stayed here, but it was purchased a few years ago and underwent a complete restoration. The approach to the Inn is grand, and the Georgian colonial structure calls out attention to detail. All reports indicate that this is a first-class establishment featuring beautifully appointed rooms and welcoming innkeepers. The website is quite comprehensive, and rates vary with a top rate of $385 per night in season. See www.StockbridgeInn.com or call 888-466-7865.

Lee

Devonfield Bed and Breakfast – Stockbridge Road

This B&B was recently purchased and renovated. The innkeepers offer nine rooms, many with wood-burning fireplaces and canopy beds. It too has the distinction of being listed as one of the original Berkshire "cottages." The public living room exudes a comfort that seems to encourage convivial conversation around the fireplace. Located across from the Grenoch Golf Club, the B&B has tennis courts and its own heated swimming pool. Rates run from $225 to $350 for the Wilhelmina Cottage. See www.Devonfield.com or call 413-243-3298.

Lenox

Garden Gables Inn – Main Street

Joel and I used to stay here when we were renovating our home. Remember? The house that kept telling us to spend money? Often I came up alone to check on things and would stay either here or at the Red Lion. The innkeepers are transplants from some big city or another, I forgot which. That seems to be a trend up here, as this is the case for every inn featured in this list. Tells us something about the nature of the Berkshires. In contrast to Christine's, which has four rooms, the Garden Gables now has nineteen rooms and suites to accommodate all levels of budget, from $165 to $375 for a weekend rate in season. Over the years new rooms and cottages have been added, so if this Inn is your pick, ask for one of the newer spots. A large outdoor pool is another blessing when the weather hits 90 degrees on some August Saturday. Garden Gables Inn is very well located, as you can walk out the door and explore Lenox. For the exercise group, the walk to Tanglewood is a mere four miles. You will need a dip in the pool after that. See www.LenoxInn.com or call 413-637-0193.

Blantyre – Lenox Road

I must admit that Blantyre is one of my favorite places; I would compare it to fine hotels anywhere in the world. We have dinner here several times a year. Just coming up the long stone driveway and glimpsing the dark red brick of this Scottish estate gets my goose bumps up. My first time at Blantyre was probably in 1982 when Joel and I stayed in a room in the newly completed carriage house. I was working as a guidance counselor and was heading up to Williamstown to chat with the director of admissions at Williams College. Somehow, I had heard of Blantyre and decided that this bit of luxury was for us. There were, however, no rooms in the main house, as an international croquet tournament was being held at Blantyre, and the entire weekend everyone was walking around in their proper croquet whites. Blantyre was spectacular then and is just as exciting now. The main house has eight rooms, all decorated to enchant the eye. The cottages and carriage house are no less inviting and offer many additional accommodations. The property boasts a pool, tennis courts, and of course that croquet court. Blantyre has added a spa to its facilities. Dining here is a most incomparable experience – something everyone should splurge on for great occasions and maybe a small occasion every once in a while as well. A romance could definitely blossom here. Room rates start at around $500. (I might add that the Fitzpatricks, who own the Red Lion Inn, also own this establishment. They know how to do things right.) See www.blantyre.com or call 413-637-3556.

Cranwell – Lee Road

This is a full-service resort. There are 105 rooms in the main house and a number of outbuildings, some of them recently constructed. This Tudor mansion is another remnant of what was know as the Gilded Age of the Berkshires. The Gilded Age brought the country's landed gentry to the area. They spent part of every summer in their palatial "cottages," many of them then moving on to their palatial "cottages" in Newport, Rhode Island. When income tax became the law of the land, the Gilded Age faded but left behind a substantial number of these cottages. Too expensive to be maintained by individual families, they often fell into disrepair and neglect. Fortunately, interested parties and investors have come along to restore these monuments to this age of excess and give all of us a chance to appreciate what was once reserved for the extraordinarily wealthy. Cranwell can be a self-contained experience, as they have a pool, tennis courts, eighteen-hole golf course and golf school, and a full-service spa and fitness center. In addition to the main dining room, there is a pub on the premises. A large ballroom and beautiful terrace make Cranwell ideal for a wedding. Our friends had their tenth anniversary party here. The food and service were excellent. Rooms start at $255 for in-season weekends and holidays. See www.cranwell.com or call 800-272-6935.

Hancock

Jiminy Peak – Corey Road

No list of hotels in the area would be complete without mentioning Jiminy Peak. An all-season resort with some very decent skiing, this is a family-friendly place catering to groups as well as individuals. Their website is so comprehensive that everything you need to know to book in will be available at the click of a mouse. See www.JiminyPeak.com or call 413-738-5500.

North Adams

The Porches Inn – 231 River Street

Another incredible venue created by the Fitzpatricks, this time Nancy Fitzpatrick. I have never been to the Porches, but by all accounts it is a place to be reckoned with. Set near Mass MoCA, the performance space and art museum constructed from abandoned warehouses in this community, Nancy Fitzpatrick's Porches Inn has fifty rooms with – according to her website – "retro-edgy, industrial granny chic ambiance which makes a spirited lodging statement…" Without having seen it, I would bet it's the most interesting and well run establishment in northern Berkshire County. In-season weekend rates around $250. See www.porches.com or call 413-664-0400.

Williamstown

The Orchards Hotel – 222 Adams Street

The drive into the courtyard is inviting. We have dinner at the Orchards Hotel from time to time, but I have never seen the rooms. Very little was available on the website, but if you are staying in northern Berkshire County, see www.OrchardsHotel.com or call 800-225-1517.

RESTAURANTS

My list of restaurants runs from blue-jeans casual to jacket-and-tie formal. The places featured here that I have eaten at are first rate, no matter what the attire. You can expect prices to go from modest to moderate to very expensive. Very expensive can be costly indeed, so check the menus on the websites to make sure you know what you are getting into before you get a bill that flattens your bankroll. This happened to us years ago in Switzerland at Freddy Giradet. They wouldn't take a credit card. We left the restaurant without a cent for cab fare, as they even took the change from Joel's pocket. Thank goodness for cash machines.

New Marlboro

The Old Inn on the Green – Route 57

This is one of my three favorite dining places in the Berkshires. So romantic to eat by candlelight in this old spot that served the itinerant traveler 150 years ago. Chef Peter is a master in the kitchen, and with James as the host and dear Jorgen as the sommelier, the Inn is just a must. Unless you are staying in Great Barrington or New Marlboro, it is a bit out of the way – from Lenox, the Old Inn is a good half-hour southeast – but absolutely worth the trip. On Wednesday and Thursday, a three-course price-fixed menu is offered for around $30, in addition to the regular menu. On Saturday night, a price-fixed menu is offered for around $65. Open only for dinner. See www.OldInn.com or call 413-229-7924.

Egremont

The Old Mill – Route 23

This is another of my three favorite eating spots and is situated in the tiny village of South Egremont. The building is an old grist mill that has been converted into a restaurant named, aptly enough, the Old Mill. You will receive the warmest welcome from Terry, your congenial host. Nights when Terry is cooking, Jennie or Christine will escort you to the bar for a few minutes while you wait for your table. Always, raucous laughter fills the packed place as Adrian pours drinks while engaging in non-stop chatter with customers. The food is excellent. And the Old Mill is one of the few restaurants that offers a salad with dinner, making this very good value for your meal. Reservations are accepted for five people or more. Call 413-528-1421.

Egremont Inn – Old Sheffield Road
This is another building from another century, with wide-plank floors and charming public spaces. The restaurant provides an eclectic menu, from a hamburger to a full dinner, with an award-winning wine list. On Thursdays and Saturdays the Inn is alive with great jazz and the dance floor sees a lot of action. See www.EgremontInn.com or call 413-528-2111.

The Elm Court – Route 71
This is where the famous Elm Court crowd hangs out. Urs Bieri's food is outstanding. I love his horseradish-crusted salmon. The bar is a favorite spot in summer as well as winter, when a wood-burning fireplace throws off an abundance of heat to warm visitors coming inside from temperatures as low as 2 degrees. Dinner can be a bit pricey but definitely worth every cent. See www.ElmCourtInn.com or call 413-528-0325.

Great Barrington
Castle Street Café – Castle Street
This is our frequent choice for a casual restaurant, with the best hamburger around. In addition to the hamburger and full dinner choices with a complimentary salad, the bar offers a more limited but equally enjoyable menu. The wine list is comprehensive, and for special dinners of ten or twelve people, chef proprietor Michael Ballon will serve dinner in the wine cellar on the lower level. Lots of great jazz in the bar. A favorite spot before and after shows at the Mahaiwe Theater next door. Reservations taken for parties of five or more. Great value for great food and service. See www.CastleStreetCafe.com or call 413-528-5244.

Pearl's – Railroad Street
At the top of the street, this contemporary take on a hip New York steak restaurant is a welcomed counterpoint to all the country restaurants in the area. There is a wonderful Sunday brunch menu. Sitting by the large windows in the bar, we look down Railroad Street, lined with small shops and eating establishments that are particular to an old New England

town. Joel and I love a hamburger, and like Castle Street, Pearl's also serves a most agreeable burger. Prices are moderate to expensive. See www.PearlsRestaurant.com or call 413-528-5244.

Aegean Breeze – Route 7
Wonderful Greek cuisine. George Cami serves a succulent grilled whole fish, a crunchy Greek salad with fresh feta cheese, and amazing desserts baked by his mother-in-law. Order a glass of Nameia, a fruity wine from Greece, to go with your dinner. When the weather permits, there is dining on the patio, and the glassed-in porch is always in season. A small fireplace in the main dining room gives us comfort when we head down here for lunch on snowy winter afternoons. This restaurant is open seven days for lunch and dinner. Moderate prices. Irene and George always honor your reservations. See www.Aegean-Breeze.com or call 413-528-4001.

Four Brothers Pizza Inn – Route 7
My grandchildren think they have not been to visit Grandma and Grandpa unless they eat at least one meal from Four Brothers. Inexpensive, family-friendly, all the usual Italian fare deliciously prepared. Good for eating in or take out. Call 413-528-9684.

Bizen – Railroad Street
We can't leave Great Barrington without mentioning the best Japanese restaurant, at least in Berkshire County. This according to sushi aficionados, which does not include me or Joel, but does include some of my very "in the know" friends and my grandson Geoffrey. This Asian establishment is owned by Michael Marcus, a man, like Geoffrey, who is apparently committed to all things Japanese. He has recently enlarged Bizen to include Kaiseki, the myriad courses which symbolize the revered tea ceremony. I must get Geoffrey up here to experience this firsthand. Below I tell you about Michael Marcus's work as a potter. He doesn't seem to have a website, but just Google Bizen and some interesting info will come up, or call 413-528-9696.
Martins – Railroad Street

This small diner-type restaurant is dedicated to breakfast and lunch. The food is good and served quickly, and the wait staff is always willing to please. Just walk in, and before you know it, hot coffee will be on your table. Call 413-528-5455.

Stockbridge

Once upon a Table – Main Street

This is our friends Charlotte and Sheldon Gross's favorite eating spot. A tiny jewel of a restaurant, its packed tables reflect excellent food and fine service. Call 413-298-3870.

The Red Lion Inn – Main Street

I think you know all about the Red Lion by now. I highly recommend the restaurant for excellent quality if not imaginative fare. The menu presents terrific New England specialties like a creamy clam chowder, and great comfort food with real turkey dinners, pot pies, and wonderful desserts. Indian pudding as well as apple pie are satisfying endings to a warm experience. On some evenings there is piano music in the side lobby, the type of music meant to soothe rather than agitate. In the summer, reservations for the outside patio are at a premium, so be sure to call 413-298-4555 a day in advance. See www.RedLionInn.com.

Lenox

Blantyre – Route 20

What more can I say about Blantyre? As you might have guessed, it is one of the trio of my favorite restaurants, and this one can compete with the best of them anywhere. Open for lunch and dinner on selected days of the week all year round. Always check the website, www.blantyre.com, or call 413-637-3556.

Napa – Church Street

This California bistro serves excellent salads, sandwiches, and main courses. The meatloaf is like Mom's, and the brisket is just as memorable.

The restaurant moved into new quarters, still on Church Street, and now has an outdoor terrace for summer dining. Call 413-637-3204.

Church Street Café – Church Street
This was the first restaurant we ate at that bitter day in 1990 when we arrived in Lenox looking for a rental. The porch was covered with snow at the time, but once summer came, Joel and I enjoyed many fine lunches and dinners on that porch. This spot has endured long after many area eateries have folded. See www.ChurchStreetCafe.biz or call 413-637-2745.

Zinc – Church Street
Owned by the same people who own Pearl's, Zinc has a decidedly sophisticated but casual air. The front room sports large windows for viewing passersby as you order lunch or dinner to eat on marble tables. The rear room has a zinc bar running its length. On weekend nights it's hard to find a space at the bar. The menu is limited, but everything is tasty and well prepared. I love the croque monsieur – with a side of crispy French fries, lunch becomes a Parisian fantasy. See www.BistroZinc.com or call 413-637-8800.

Café Lucia – Church Street
This café has been a mainstay for Italian food for as long as I can remember. Pleasant atmosphere and outdoor dining in season on the deck. Not a place we frequent, but friends eat there consistently and love it. Call 413-637-2640.

Prime – Franklin Street
Prime is a relatively new steak restaurant. We ate here when it first opened; and while the food was very good, the prices were hefty but the portions were not. The atmosphere is New York chic. It looks like a lot of thought went into the ambiance, and I am willing to give it another try with the hope that the offerings have become more substantial. Don't mind the prices, but you're supposed to leave a steak place feeling like

you are going to explode. Sounds a little disgusting, but it's true, at least for Joel. Call 413-637-2998.

Pittsfield

Spice – North Street

This is a gorgeous restaurant laid out with beautiful mahogany accents. There are three dining areas serving eclectic American fare. One night on the spur of the moment, Joel and I had a very good meal at the bar. We went back several weeks later with our neighbors and we were disappointed as the food was not nearly as flavorful as the first time. It is a new restaurant and we will try it again. I guess it can take time to get the kinks out. See www.Spice-Restaurant.com or call 413-443-1234.

Williamstown

The Mill on the Floss – Route 7

Specializing in fine French food, this restaurant has been servicing patrons for many years and manages to keep up quality and service. We have eaten in the lovely paneled dining room on occasion when going to the Williamstown Theatre Festival. Never disappoints. See www.MillOnTheFloss.com or call 413-458-9123.

The Orchards Hotel – Adams Road

Yasmin's restaurant is another great dining spot in this small college town. Each summer we meet our friends the Shaws to attend the latest exhibits at the Clark Museum, and we always finish the day off with an early dinner at this hotel. There is an inviting garden, but when we go we seem to pick the worst weather and wind up eating inside. Maybe next year we'll get lucky. See www.OrchardsHotel.com or call 413-455-1977.

THEATER

You will be surprised at the professional level of theater in Berkshire County. Each one of the many houses seems to provide us with an extraordinary level of quality material, as evidenced by the number of shows that are first performed here and then wind up in New York City.

Berkshire Theatre Festival – Stockbridge
Not really a festival, the Berkshire Theatre Festival is one of the country's premiere summer stock venues, located in the center of Stockbridge. It has been packing in seasonal tourists and locals for seventy-eight years. An extraordinary number of the finest actors have graced this stage: JoAnne Woodward and Richard Chamberlin are in a list too numerous to mention. The BTF has had its share of productions head for successful runs in New York City. The main stage is augmented by the smaller Unicorn Theatre, both offering quality plays from late spring into late fall. See www.BerkshireTheatre.org or call 413-298-5576.

Shakespeare and Company – Lenox
You will find this outstanding repertory theater in Lenox, a short ride north of Stockbridge. Launched thirty years ago by its visionary director Tina Packer, Shakespeare and Company offers more than just the Bard. A drama as superb as *Golda's Balcony* found its way from Lenox to a long run on Broadway. The woman who played Golda in the Company production put on an outstanding performance, but I suppose Tova Feldshuh was cast for the New York stage because of name recognition. This and other new works, along with short plays by Edith Wharton and other well established playwrights, live side by side with performances of Shakespeare's comedies, tragedies, and histories. The Founder's Theatre will soon be joined by an exact replica of London's Rose Theatre, where Shakespeare's original plays were performed. I love taking guests to the July 4th public reading of the Declaration of Independence. I am always blinking back tears. This company should not be missed. See www.shakespeare.org or call 413-637-1199.

Barrington Stage Company – Pittsfield
Coming into its twelfth year, Barrington Stage has enhanced the area's theater choices. Once again, outstanding revivals as well as superior new works seem to be commonplace to this company, which left the high school auditorium in Sheffield to purchase its own theater in Pittsfield. *Spelling*

Bee originated with Barrington Stage, and its Broadway success is verging on legendary. See www.BarringtonStageCo.org or call 413-236-8888.

Williamstown Theatre Festival – Williamstown

This completes the group of larger theater companies in the area, although there are many smaller arenas where local works are performed and plays read. The Williamstown Theatre Festival celebrates classics as well as new plays all summer. Located amidst the Greek revival buildings of beautiful Williams College, this company also offers summer workshops, cabarets, and special events. See www.wtfestival.org or call 413-597-3377.

MUSIC

While the Berkshires is famous for its abundance of classical music, you should be aware that jazz, rock, folk, and alternative music are alive and flourishing here as well. Even Tanglewood hosts such popular artists as James Taylor and jazz greats like John Pizzereli. There is certainly something for everyone.

Aston Magna Concerts – Great Barrington

These concerts take place at the Daniel Arts Center of Simon's Rock College. In its thirty-fifth season, this is the country's oldest summer festival of music performed on period instruments. See www.AstonMagna.org or call 800-875-7156.

Stockbridge Chamber Concerts – Great Barrington

Concerts are held each summer Monday evening at Searles Castle. Distinguished musicians, many from the Boston Symphony, bring a superb caliber of classical music to this intriguing venue. See www.StockbridgeChamberConcerts.org.

Close Encounters with Music – location varies

This is one of my favorite musical experiences and has been for the fifteen years Yehuda Hanani has sought to educate and delight audiences with his world class chamber music concerts. Close Encounters with Music performances have been held in venues as diverse as the Norman Rockwell

Museum, St. James Church, and lately Mahaiwe Theater. The annual concert takes place Memorial Day weekend at Ozawa Hall of Tanglewood. Hanani, a superb cellist, begins each evening with an informative description and occasional anecdotes about the music we are going to hear. Each event is followed by a reception at which time we can partake of hors d'oeuvres and conversation with the musicians. Performances take place between October and May. See www.cewm.org.

Berkshire Bach Society – Great Barrington
The Society provides the Berkshires with quality concerts from fall to late spring. The signature performance for me is the New Year's Eve concert showcasing the six Brandenburg concertos. With the Berkshires dressed in a snowy white blanket and bright Christmas lights sparkling from tree limbs, friends fill the auditorium at the Mahaiwe Theater to capacity. The six o'clock performance is always a joyous precursor to the celebrations to follow. See www.BerkshireBach.org.

Tanglewood – Lenox
So much has been written about Tanglewood in this book, it seems redundant to go through it again. The season runs for eight weeks from early July to the end of August. The most comprehensive guide to performances, times, ticket prices, etc., is on the website. See www.bso.org.

The Egremont Inn – Egremont
Castle Street Café– Great Barrington
Helsinki Café – Great Barrington
The Guthrie Center – Great Barrington
The Lion's Den at the Red Lion Inn – Stockbridge
These establishments provide a variety of musical experiences. Jazz, alternative music, folk music, and country music are available almost nightly during season at one venue or another. Check their websites and you will find all you need to know to get your fill of any kind of musical experience. Or see www.BerkshireEagle.com for the weekly entertainment schedule.

ANTIQUES

Route 7 is all you need to know to find any and all types of antiques, from the whimsical to the fabulous. A few of my favorite places follow as we move south on Route 7 from Great Barrington towards Sheffield.

Olde Antiques

Great browsing and very affordable. We bought our old pine grandfather clock here many years ago. This establishment used to be on Route 7 at what was the Jenifer Commons but has moved to Route 7, south of Great Barrington. Lots of wonderful glassware and other objects of interest to the collector.

Elise Abrams

Bring a fat checkbook, as this store is not for the fainthearted. Featuring gorgeous antique dishes, glasses, and all that works for a fabulous table setting, Elyse Abrams' is worth wandering through. Who knows, maybe that perfectly etched candy dish is waiting for you. See www.EliseAbrams.com or call 413-528-3201.

The Country Dining Room

This shop also displays exquisite antiques for setting the fantasy dining table. Sheila Chavetz's glassware, silver, and dishes grace fine tables that are for sale. She and her husband have a selection of linens and napkins rings that my friends seem to purchase by the dozen each time they visit. The huge display of English transfer ware is a draw for me, as I decided that a wall of these beautiful old plates was preferable to paintings above our dining room sideboard. The second floor has items equally beautiful but of a more rustic quality. Love this shop. See www.CountryDiningRoomAntiq.com or call 413-528-5050.

Susan Silver

You'll find very elegant European furniture here. Joel loves Susan's tufted leather chairs and leather tooled desks. See www.SusanSilverAntiques.com or call 413-229-8169.

Le Trianon
This is a large establishment filled with furniture and artwork, I believe, exclusively from France. See www.LeTrianonAntiques.com or call 413-528-0775.

GALLERIES

As with the antique stores, there are too many galleries in the Berkshires to name, but I will share a couple of my favorites with you.

The Witt Gallery – Lenox
Located in the heart of town, the gallery has an interesting mix of contemporary and avant-garde artwork. See www.TheWittGallery.com or call 413-637-8808.

The Hoadley Gallery – Lenox
This gallery specializes in American crafts including pottery, jewelry, and clothing. See www.HoadleyGallery.com or call 413-637-2814.

Charles L. Flint – Lenox
This gallery shows not only extraordinary American and European paintings but also very fine American folk art and antiques as well. A while back *Architectural Digest* devoted several pages to this gallery. Most of what you will find here is museum quality so, once again, bring a fat checkbook. See www.flint.com or call 413-637-1634.

Lascano Gallery – Great Barrington
This Main Street gallery features fairly large contemporary works. See www.LascanoGallery.com or call 413-528-0471.

The Loring Gallery – Sheffield
My favorite gallery, of course, located on Route 7. Anne, Rosemary, and Natalie seem to fill this space with every piece of artwork I could possibly love. The sculpture isn't chopped liver either. Remember, if you are a

serious buyer, get there in time for lunch. See www.LoringGallery.com or call 413-229-0110.

Joyous Spring Pottery – Monterey

Remember Michael Marcus from Bizen restaurant? Do yourself a favor and visit his home/studio. I took a friend there several years ago; it was one of the more interesting things we did that weekend. We were asked to remove our shoes, Japanese style, and entered a quiet, peaceful room. After watching a short video showing how the artist works and fires his pieces in the kiln behind the studio, we were amazed by the beauty of his display. Call 413-528-4115.

VENUES

There are a few places of interest that defy a specific category but are worth mentioning. The word "theater" in some of the following does not denote traditional play performances but rather eclectic offerings to suit different tastes.

The Mahaiwe Theater – Great Barrington

Lola Jaffee was the driving force behind a much needed restoration of this 102-year-old theater. At its inception the 1,000-seat auditorium hosted traveling Broadway shows, vaudeville, and movies. Currently the schedule is once again filled with a variety of exciting performers almost weekly all year round. See www.mahaiwe.org.

The Colonial Theatre – Pittsfield

This venue fell into disuse and disrepair more than half a century ago. The site was the home of a retail store until its restoration and subsequent rededication as a performing arts center. Committed to a yearly calendar, the Colonial has been part of the revitalization of Pittsfield. See www.TheColonialTheatre.org.

Mass MoCA – North Adams

MoCA is an acronym for Museum of Contemporary Art. This venue is the result of extensive renovation of old warehouse space. It has become one of the premier showcases for new art in the United States. Not just an art museum, it offers many performance events. The website describes Mass MoCA as "a welcoming place that encourages dynamic interchange between making and presenting art, between the visual and performing arts, and between the historic campus and the patrons, workers, and tenants who inhabit it." See www.MassMoCA.org.

Jacobs Pillow for Dance – Becket
Located about half an hour east of Stockbridge, Jacobs Pillow is home of the oldest dance festival in the country. The season runs from late June into late August and features premier dance companies from around the world. In addition to the regular schedule, a list of free events is also available. See www.JacobsPillow.org.

MUSEUMS

Because museums give life to the past, the ones listed below will enhance your current experience in the Berkshires by adding to your understanding of some of its history. Names we have heard throughout a lifetime – artists and authors and composers – have all found value in pursuing their craft here in this remarkably receptive environment.

Norman Rockwell Museum – Stockbridge
This building, designed by the noted architect Robert A.M. Stern, houses the largest collection of Rockwell's original artwork. In addition to the Museum's primary focus on Rockwell, curator Laurie Moffat brings to Stockbridge an eclectic mix of interesting exhibits by other artists. I have found this to be a child-friendly place where my grandchildren have learned tolerance through Rockwell's work. I remember Danielle being so moved by the poster of the little black girl having tomatoes thrown at her as she tried to enter an all-white school during the civil rights struggles of the 1950s and '60s. This is a definite go-to activity. See www.nrm.org.

Chesterwood – Stockbridge

Practically around the corner from the Rockwell, Chesterwood is the home of noted sculptor Daniel Chester French. You can tour his studio and see replicas of the famous Minute Man statue as well as a replica of French's work the Lincoln Memorial. Of course, the original is in Washington, D.C. Every time we go to D.C. and see it, both Joel and I are visibly emotional. See www.chesterwood.org.

The Mount – Lenox

Home of Edith Wharton and, for a long time, Shakespeare and Company, the Mount is now in the final stages of a complete restoration. On Mondays at four o'clock in the summer, the Mount sponsors a Women of Achievement lecture series, calling attention to those women who have impacted society through their literary, artistic, and humanitarian works. I love this series. By the way, it is not for women only. Quite a number of men attend these lectures. See www.EdithWharton.org.

Arrowhead – Pittsfield

Arrowhead was the home of Herman Melville during the time he wrote his signature epic *Moby Dick*. I have never been there, but it is probably time for me to check this one out. If you have been caught by the story of Captain Ahab and the great white whale, this may be a destination of choice for you. See www.MobyDick.org or call 413-442-1793.

Berkshire Museum – Pittsfield

This small gem of a museum is so child friendly that it is often a favorite destination when my grandkids are here. The museum has a terrific aquarium and during Christmas the exhibit of creative holiday trees is a visual treat. Additionally all summer the Little Cinema shows terrific art films as well as first run features. See www.BerkshireMuseum.org.

Francine and Sterling Clark Museum – Williamstown

We delight in meeting our friends the Shaws at least once a summer in Williamstown. This museum's fabulous exhibits of American and

European art, especially French impressionists, are always worth the hour's ride we each take in order to meet here. We have also come up for some excellent concerts. Danielle, who plays the flute, took a ride with us one Sunday to be entertained by a fine flutist. See www.ClarkArt.edu or call 413-458-2303.

Hancock Shaker Village – Hancock

Not your typical museum, this restored village is dedicated to the now extinct community of Shakers who lived here almost a century ago. Here, in a space alive with activity, you will see re-creations of everyday life as well as displays of Shaker furniture and other crafts of the time. See www.HancockShakerVillage.org.

SPAS

Promoted as luxurious necessities, spas seem to be springing up everywhere. In addition to organizations specifically dedicated to health, fitness, and the general care and feeding of our bodies and psyches, hotels have entered the spa arena, creating such spaces to accommodate the needs of their guests. Below is a mix of dedicated spas and hotel spa facilities.

Canyon Ranch – Lenox

Like the Red Lion Inn, much has been described about Canyon Ranch. Go to www.CanyonRanch.com. You will be rewarded with current info and a strong feel for the ranch.

Cranwell – Lenox

Cranwell offers full spa services and a fitness center in a clean and spacious environment. It is good for me, because, unlike at Canyon Ranch, I can book in for one service or bring our guests for a day. See www.Cranwell.com.

Mepal Spa – New Marlboro

This newest spa is about ten minutes south of Great Barrington. It's a full-service spa, but the last time we were there, they didn't have a fitness center. I love the place. Being on the small side, it feels tranquil, and again the option to book in for one or two services is just what we need on a nasty day. They sometimes offer lunch in the mansion on request. If you can get it, this is a great follow-up to your spa experience. See www.MepalSpa.com.

Kripalu Center for Yoga and Health – Stockbridge
Kripalu is unlike anything else described above. Based on the philosophy of yoga, the retreat – with its spare rooms where you make your own bed – is dedicated to the health, well being, and healing of the total person. See www.kripalu.org.

HIKING
Hiking is always a favorite activity for guests. Below are just a few of the possibilities. Get a book on hiking (and biking) in the Berkshires for a comprehensive guide.

Monument Mountain – Great Barrington
I am not much into hiking, but most of our guests and each of our kids and grandkids enjoy this climb each time they visit. Our guests' commitment to this hike – moderate to moderately difficult depending on which trail you take – becomes my precious time alone for an hour or two.

Mt. Greylock – North Adams
We have driven up to the peak of Mt. Greylock. Reaching an altitude of almost 3,500 feet, this would be a long and difficult hike. I much prefer to see the incredible 360-degree view after we get out of our car. According to a website called www.AmericasRoof.com, Mt. Greylock has been an inspiration for famous authors and artists. This website is worth looking at, but the official website is www.mass.gov/dcr/parks/western/mgry.htm. Check for the reopening of the road to the summit, as restrictions might be in place to due road reconstruction.

Bash Bish Falls – Mt. Washington
Part of a cluster of state parks, Bash Bish Falls in Mt. Washington boasts thirty miles of hiking trails and the most dramatic waterfalls in Massachusetts. See www.mass.gov/dcr/parks/western/bash.htm.

GOLF

Public golf is limited to the couple of courses below, but if you need your fix on the links, just pack your clubs and indulge. There is so much to do around here, I don't know why people would choose to spend a day aggravating themselves with those sticks, which I have dubbed my weapons of mass destruction.

Egremont Country Club – Egremont
This club offers a semi-private eighteen-hole course located on Route 23. For rates and availability of tee times, log onto www.EgermontCountryClub.com.

Cranwell – Lenox
This public facility offers a challenging eighteen-hole course, a comprehensive golf school, and a driving range. See www.cranwell.com.

Greenock – Lee
This nine-hole semi-private course was designed by the famous Donald Ross. A scenic and challenging day of golf awaits you when you reserve your tee time. See www.greenockcc.com.

WATER SPORTS

The Berkshires has myriad lakes for non-motorized and motorized boats. Most of the lakes have a public boat ramp. We like to take kayaks to a small lake around the corner from us where the kids can spend the day swimming and boating.

Boat Rental

You can go to Lake Pontoosic in Pittsfield to rent boats by the day. Call 413-442-7020.

White Water Rafting
A company called Crab Apple arranges white water rafting trips in Berkshire County. See www.CrabAppleInc.com.

The Stockbridge Bowl
Also known as Lake Mackinac, the Stockbridge Bowl may be the most famous lake up here. Its visibility from Tanglewood is particularly prized on nights when fireworks are displayed from the lake itself. Wintertime find kids iceskating and fisherman sitting on the frozen surface sinking their poles into holes in the ice hoping for a catch. In summer the small bungalows on the Bowl have served as the perfect seasonal home for many members of the Boston Symphony. The public beach is public for Stockbridge residents only, but anyone can drop their canoe or kayak into the Bowl from the public boat ramp.

SKIING
There are a number of ski areas functioning all winter. The easiest way to decide where you want to ski is to explore www.BerkshireSkiing.com, where all pertinent information is available.

Catamount – Hillsdale, New York
Probably the largest mountain in the Southern Berkshires, Catamount is on Route 23. See www.CatamountSki.com or call 518-325-3200.

Butternut Basin – Great Barrington
Further up, east on Route 23 is Butternut, where my family takes to the slopes. See www.SkiButternut.com or call 413-528-2000.

Bosquet – on the Lenox/Pittsfield line
North on Route 7, Bosquet is small but very family friendly. See www.bosquet.com or call 413-442-8316.

Jiminy Peak – North County
Still further up Route 7, Jiminy Peak probably has the best conditions in the Berkshires. See www.JiminyPeak.com or call 413-738-5500.

ETCETERA

The book includes a number of miscellaneous places that are useful to know about. The following details those spots as well as some not specifically mentioned.

Benmarl Winery – Marlboro, New York
The oldest farm winery in the country, this spot is a delightful weekend getaway. Mark Miller sold the place a few years ago, and it is now under new management but just as delightful as ever. Wine is available for tasting every day, and you still may bring a picnic for lunch overlooking the lush Hudson Valley. See www. benmarl.com.

Boscobel – Route 9W north approaching Cold Spring
This small beautiful mansion restoration is open for tours and in the summer hosts the Hudson Valley Shakespeare Festival on the grounds. Coupled with the charming town of Cold Spring, this makes for another great weekend visit. See www.boscobel.org.

Guido's Market – one on the Lenox/Pittsfield line, one in Great Barrington
Remember Balducci's in lower Manhattan? Well, this is our answer to that fabulous specialty market that carries the finest of everything you will need to put an out-of-this-world meal on those dishes you bought at the Country Dining Room. See www.GuidosFreshMarketPlace.com or call 413-528-4488.

Our Daily Bread – Great Barrington and Stockbridge
Remember those split baguettes we cut for our picnics and luncheons? The only place to get really good French bread is in this bakery, housed in a small market called Gorham and Norton in Great Barrington, or in

their satellite shop in Stockbridge. I can taste the crunch as I am writing. The number for Gorham and Norton is 413-528-0900.

Taft Farm – Great Barrington
I can't say enough about Martha's pies, but that is not all. In season Taft Farm's strawberries and fresh-from-the-field corn are mind-blowing. The corn needs nothing but your own teeth; take a bite and tender kernels explode with summer's sweetness. (I never realized that eating corn is a personal style. Joel munches across the cob like a typewriter – remember those? – and I eat it any which way it hits my mouth. This makes him nuts.) Martha also makes great sandwiches to fill your Tanglewood basket. See www.TaftFarms.com or call 413-528-1515.

SoCo Creamery – Great Barrington, Lenox, and Stockbridge
What used to be Bev's Ice Cream is now called SoCo Creamery. This local ice cream parlor started as one small store developed by an actual Bev. Not only did she have the creamiest ice cream but also the best chocolate cake I've ever tasted. I remember literally stuffing chocolate cake into my mouth even before I got out of the store. Bev's was taken over a couple of years ago, I believe, by her sons – hence the name change. Still superb ice cream. Call 413-528-9420.

Nejaime's Wines Cellars – Stockbridge, Lenox, and Pittsfield
Jack, in the Stockbridge store, is your man for picking out the perfect wine for your occasion. The shops carry a fine selection of cheeses and breads to go with that wine, and will prepare a great feast for your Tanglewood picnic.

Country Curtains – Stockbridge
I love this shop. The one in Stockbridge is located on the lower level of the Red Lion Inn. Not surprising, as Country Curtains is also the genius of the Fitzpatrick family. They have stores from as far south as Virginia through the northeast into Massachusetts. I have managed to purchase curtains, bedding, and other household items there for each of

our homes in the Berkshires since we first rented in 1991. The quality is exceptional for ready-made items and the prices won't destroy your budget. Explore their on-line catalogue at www.CountryCurtains.com. Feel free to browse around the store when you get up to the Berkshires.

Bridlewood – Rt. 7 in Great Barrington
Shannon Bronwyn has an eclectic collection of country furniture that would enhance any Berkshire house. Often, I can't pass there after my food shop at the Price Chopper without stopping in to see what's new. In addition to furniture, she has a wide array of gift items and charming accessories for the home.

Wingate – Rt. 7 in Great Barrington
Valerie and staff have excellent taste for those decorating a residence in a grand style. I have admired the home of our friends in Monterey who trusted Wingate to assist with the interior design as well as furnishing and accessorizing down to the last detail.

Well, now you have enough to do to keep you busy for a weekend, a month or, like Joel and me, a lifetime. We love it here. You will too. See you in the Berkshires!

BOOK ORDER FORM

If you enjoyed reading *Having Guests Means Never Seeing the View,* send a gift copy to a friend for any occasion, or as a recent guest send this book as a thank you to your hosts.

Merry Hill Press will be pleased to post your order with an enclosed message. Simply fill out the form below. Mail the form with a check for $14.00 plus $4.00 for shipping to each individual address. (For more than one book to an address, shipping is $2.00 per book.) Please reprint this form for each book shipped to a different address.

Checks should be paid to the order of:
Merry Hill Press
P.O. Box 341
Great Barrington, MA 01230

Your Name ____

Your Address____

Your Tel and E-mail____

Send to:
Name ____

Address ____

Tel____

Message____

____

____

Thank you for your order.